GUIDELINES

VOL 33 / PART 2
May–August 2017

Commissioned by **David Spriggs** | Edited by **Lisa Cherrett**

The Bible Reading Fellowship
15 The Chambers, Vineyard
Abingdon OX14 3FE
brf.org.uk

The Bible Reading Fellowship (BRF) is a Registered Charity (233280)

ISBN 978 0 85746 445 3

Cover image © Hisham Ibrahim/PhotoV/Alamy

Distributed in Australia by:
MediaCom Education Inc, PO Box 610, Unley, SA 5061
Tel: 1 800 811 311 | admin@mediacom.org.au

Distributed in New Zealand by:
Scripture Union Wholesale, PO Box 760, Wellington
Tel: 04 385 0421 | suwholesale@clear.net.nz

Acknowledgements
The New Revised Standard Version of the Bible, Anglicised Edition, copyright © 1989, 1995 by the Division of Christian Education of the National Council of the Churches of Christ in the USA. Used by permission. All rights reserved.

The Holy Bible, New International Version, Anglicised edition, copyright © 1979, 1984, 2011 by Biblica. Used by permission of Hodder & Stoughton Publishers, an Hachette UK company. All rights reserved. 'NIV' is a registered trademark of Biblica. UK trademark number 1448790.

Printed by Gutenberg Press, Tarxien, Malta

Suggestions for using *Guidelines*

Set aside a regular time and place, if possible, when you can read and pray undisturbed. Before you begin, take time to be still and, if you find it helpful, use the BRF Prayer on page 6.

In *Guidelines*, the introductory section provides context for the passages or themes to be studied, while the units of comment can be used daily, weekly, or whatever best fits your timetable. You will need a Bible (more than one if you want to compare different translations) as Bible passages are not included. At the end of each week is a 'Guidelines' section, offering further thoughts about, or practical application of what you have been studying.

Occasionally, you may read something in *Guidelines* that you find particularly challenging, even uncomfortable. This is inevitable in a series of notes which draws on a wide spectrum of contributors, and doesn't believe in ducking difficult issues. Indeed, we believe that *Guidelines* readers much prefer thought-provoking material to a bland diet that only confirms what they already think.

If you do disagree with a contributor, you may find it helpful to go through these three steps. First, think about why you feel uncomfortable. Perhaps this is an idea that is new to you, or you are not happy at the way something has been expressed. Or there may be something more substantial—you may feel that the writer is guilty of sweeping generalisation, factual error, theological or ethical misjudgment. Second, pray that God would use this disagreement to teach you more about his word and about yourself. Third, think about what you will do as a result of the disagreement. You might resolve to find out more about the issue, or write to the contributor or the editors of *Guidelines*.

To send feedback, you may email or write to BRF at the addresses shown opposite. If you would like your comment to be included on our website, please email connect@brf.org.uk. You can also Tweet to @brfonline, using the hashtag #brfconnect.

Writers in this issue

Kate Bruce is Deputy Warden at Cranmer Hall Durham, where she teaches preaching at BA and MA level. She did her PhD on preaching and imagination and has written a number of books and articles on this area. She seeks to encourage and develop excellence in preaching and communication.

Margaret Guite is an Anglican priest and Team Rector of a group of parishes in south-east Cambridgeshire. She has taught Doctrine at Westcott House and Wesley House in Cambridge, and has served in a variety of parishes in the Diocese of Ely. She is an Honorary Canon of Ely Cathedral.

David Kerrigan first joined BMS in 1983 and served in countries including Bangladesh and Sri Lanka, interspersed with periods of study and church leadership in the UK. He has been General Director of BMS World Mission since 2009.

Nigel G. Wright was Principal of Spurgeon's College from 2000 to 2013 and is a former President of the Baptist Union of Great Britain. He has written *Jesus Christ—the Alpha and the Omega* for BRF (2010).

David Spriggs has retired from Bible Society but continues his work with them as a consultant. His main role is as a team minister at the Hinckley Baptist Church, with special responsibility to work with the leaders.

John Leach is Developing Discipleship Adviser and Trainer in the Diocese of Lincoln. He was previously the vicar of St John's, Folkestone, and is a trainer, liturgist and musician. He has also worked as Director of Anglican Renewal Ministries.

Meg Warner is a Teaching Fellow at King's College London and a Reader in the Church of England. She travels around the UK and internationally, talking about the Bible, and especially the Old Testament. Meg Warner is the author of SPCK's 2016 Lent Book, *Abraham: A journey through Lent*.

Keith Neville is a teacher of Religious Studies in a secondary school in Rugby. He is an ordained minister who has served in three Baptist churches across the country and is currently engaged in doctoral research into the epistle of James and its early church context.

P.W. (Bill) Goodman encourages and enables lifelong learning among church leaders in the Anglican Diocese of Lincoln. *Yearning for You*, a conversation between biblical songs and contemporary songs about desire for intimacy, is the published version of his Sheffield PhD.

David Spriggs writes...

This issue of *Guidelines* covers the Christian festival of Pentecost, when we remember the outpouring of God's Spirit on the early church. The Holy Spirit is central for understanding how God communicates with us. It is helpful, therefore, that Kate Bruce, who works as a theologian in Durham with a special interest in the way we communicate God's truth in our culture, looks at the varied ways in which God communicates in the Bible.

David Kerrigan, who has spent his life in mission work, concludes his series helping us to grasp more clearly the missiological significance of the life of Jesus by exploring the way the Holy Spirit deepens the challenge of mission. Keith Neville takes us further as he delves into mission in John's Gospel. Mission is a thread that runs through this Gospel, not confined to the well-known 'Paraclete' passages.

Intimately connected to the mission of the church and the work of the Holy Spirit is discipleship. John Leach brings his very varied life experience to bear on the challenges to discipleship today. You can discover why the Bible matters to John in his additional article.

Matthew was concerned to communicate God's truth to his readers, and Nigel Wright continues his insights on Matthew as he explores chapters 19—23.

The Old Testament makes an important contribution in this issue. Maggie Guite expounds the messages of the prophets Joel and Haggai, bringing both scholarship and pastoral sensitivity to the task. I unpack the importance of the book of Amos, another of the twelve 'minor prophets'. Amos is especially important as the first of the 'writing prophets' but also for the substantial contribution he makes to our understanding of social justice. Meg Warner then helps us appreciate the many ways in which the account of Abraham's life we find in Genesis has spoken to God's people.

'Happiness' is a topic that fascinates many people. Andy Parnham has engaged with this interest by writing a bridge-building course. I offer, with his support, some biblical background to his approach.

The Song of Solomon explores the 'happiness' and pain of love. Bill Goodman concludes this issue by bringing the insights he has gained through studying the text of the Song of Solomon alongside some contemporary lyrics. These songs are full of metaphors about the beauty and challenges of intimate love between a man and a woman.

I hope, by now, you can't wait to get into this issue of *Guidelines*!

The BRF Prayer

Almighty God,
you have taught us that your word is a lamp for our feet
and a light for our path. Help us, and all who prayerfully
read your word, to deepen our fellowship with you
and with each other through your love.
And in so doing may we come to know you more fully,
love you more truly, and follow more faithfully
in the steps of your son Jesus Christ, who lives and reigns
with you and the Holy Spirit, one God for evermore.
Amen

The communicating God

Central to faith, mission, leadership, discipleship, prayer and preaching is the conviction that God communicates. From prophetic utterances to commandments carved in stone, the Bible reveals in myriad ways the communicative nature of God. In the story of Jacob we meet the God who takes us seriously, even in our fear and foolishness. He understands reticence in leaders and equips us for the tasks ahead, as we see with the example of Moses. God communicates through human creativity; this is exemplified in the artistic talents he imparts to Bezalel and Oholiab. In Nathan's parable we see God inhabiting carefully constructed language to bring about penitence. Divine communication can be earthed, grounded and practical, as we see in the hands-on angelic care for Elijah, as well as awesome, holy and overwhelmingly 'other', as Isaiah's vision in the temple exemplifies.

Throughout both Testaments the Bible often places the divine voice in the mouth of angelic emissaries, who appear to surprising people, bringing remarkable messages (Genesis 21:15–19; Luke 2:8–20). There are no boundaries to God's communicative desire; astrologers recognise the star as part of a communicative act. 'Outsiders' like Na'aman the Syrian and the widow of Zarephath receive his healing and provision. God redraws boundaries to make the outsider the insider. God is not the director who stands aside from the play; he steps on to the stage: Jesus Christ is God's ultimate speech-act. In the parables God communicates through compressed wisdom that captures the imagination (Luke 15:8–10). Even the cry of Jesus from the cross (Mark 15:34) points us to the presence of the silent other, vindicated in the dawning light of resurrection (John 20:1–18).

The aim of these notes is to explore some of the myriad ways in which God communicates, seeking to delight, discipline, engage and enable his people.

Quotations are taken from the New Revised Standard Version.

1 God of the wrestling

Genesis 32:22–32; John 21:15–19

The truth that God engages with us in our struggles is depicted beautifully in today's passage. Jacob's story is a tale of dysfunctional relationships, favouritism and deception. God reaches out to this wheeler-dealer of the ancient world, appearing in a dream and promising him descendants (Genesis 28:10–15). Jacob the deceiver is sensitive to God (Genesis 28:16–22). His story bursts the bounds of tidy lines where 'good' people are in and 'bad' people out.

We meet Jacob on his way back to Canaan, where his brother Esau lives. Many years have passed since he stole Esau's blessing, but, in relation to family feuds, time is not necessarily a healer. Jacob journeys home because God has told him to return (Genesis 31:3). The camera zooms in on Jacob alone at the ford of the River Jabbok. It is night. Without warning, a mysterious assailant springs on to the scene and matches Jacob shove for shove, block for block, blow for blow, until daybreak.

After this night of wrestling, the enigmatic figure puts Jacob's hip out of its socket. Still Jacob hangs on: 'I will not let you go unless you bless me' (v. 26). Last time Jacob sought a blessing, he was in disguise (Genesis 27:15–16). Now he is stripped down, confessing that he is 'Jacob', a name that means 'deceiver'. The mysterious warrior renames him 'Israel, for you have striven with God' (v. 28). Jacob names the place 'Peniel', meaning 'the face of God'. The narrative points us to the assailant's divine identity and Israel limps away, marked by this blessed and painful encounter.

Later, on a beach by a lake, just after daybreak, another flawed, frightened and foolish man meets God. Peter and Jesus wrestle with words (John 21:15–19) as Peter the denier is given opportunity to express his love and know divine restoration.

We may disguise our naked need for God and seek solace in that which is not God. Yet, if we listen to the longing below the muddled desires, we will come to the place where our desire and God's longing meet. The wonder of it is that at this 'ford' we encounter the God who takes us seriously, wrestling with us and blessing us.

2 God equips

Exodus 4:10–15; Acts 2:14–41

In the verses preceding today's passage, we see Moses offer three objections to God's instruction to go to Pharaoh and bring the Israelites out of Egypt: 'Who am I?' (Exodus 3:11), 'Who are you?' (3:13), and 'They won't believe me' (4:1). A fourth is added in verse 10: 'I'm not eloquent.' God meets all of Moses's objections, equipping him with knowledge, signs of power and reassurance. But none of this is enough to convince Moses that he is able to face Pharaoh and, with refreshing honesty, he bursts out, 'O my Lord, please send someone else' (v. 13).

Moses' fear is understandable, but it reveals a lack of trust in God as one who is infinitely more powerful than Pharaoh. God has demonstrated that he can enable Moses, but Moses' fear frames the situation so that all he can see is difficulty. In response to his reluctance we read the uncomfortable line, 'The anger of the Lord was kindled against Moses' (v. 14). The verb 'kindled' recalls the burning bush, another signifier of the power of God that Moses has witnessed. In his anger, God does not turn away from Moses but points to Aaron, who will act as a mouthpiece for Moses. God will not permit Moses' sense of his own inadequacy to prevent him from exercising the leadership to which he has been called: 'I will be with your mouth and with his mouth, and will teach you what you shall do' (v. 15).

We see a similar enabling of a flawed human in Peter when he addresses a crowd, some of whom are sneering derisively, with words of theological conviction, scriptural understanding and spiritual power, such that 3000 people are converted (Acts 2:14–41). This is all the more remarkable when we recall that Peter, frightened of the consequences of being recognised as one of Jesus' followers, denied him (Luke 22:55–62). Now we see him preaching boldly in a public context. In Peter we see 'the grace of office' exemplified—the gracious enabling that causes people to lead with courage and confidence, grounded in God.

There is great encouragement here for all who are called by God to rise to new challenges. The communicating God is the enabling God.

3 God communicates beyond words

Exodus 35:30—36:2

Picture the scene: an open space filled with piles of colourful yarns, rolls of fine linen, a heap of glittering gemstones, a pile of acacia wood. One person is hammering out gold, while another works in silver. Someone is cutting precious stones; another weaves threads into a beautiful cloth. There are designers thinking and sketching, and people working in wood, measuring, carving, sawing and fixing. Bezalel and Oholiab move about among them, stopping, pointing, talking and teaching. This is a gathering of people creating a place of encounter, full of beauty, splashed with colour and intricate design—a holy place, full of holy things. God breathes life into the art, and such art points back to God.

The source of Bezalel's and Oholiab's creative skill is directly linked with an infilling with the Spirit of God (35:31); it is God who gives artistic skill (35:35—36:2). God communicates beyond words, through the sensory richness of artistry, inspiring Bezalel and Oholiab to teach others every kind of craft.

Where are your places of artistically inspired encounter with God? Take Durham Cathedral. It conveys a strong sense of majesty. As you move from the nave into the quire, towards the high altar, there is a sense of the holiness and otherness of God. It is hard not to be aware of your littleness as your eye takes in the enormous carved pillars and soaring arches. Cuthbert's shrine conveys a sense of intimacy; Fenwick Lawson's *Pieta* speaks powerfully of bereavement and hope, death and resurrection. Beautiful voices wrap around each other in harmony as the choir sings the anthem, communicating complexity, depth and richness. Sunlight streams through the narratives in stained glass, creating dappled patches of moving light.

Perhaps our faith can be too cerebral, full of cool abstraction. Sometimes we use language that flattens out wonder, making it seem as if God can be neatly boxed. Today's passage reminds us that God is the God of technicolour, speaking through a variety of artistic media. God breathes life into art, and such art points back to God.

4 God speaks through the craft of language

2 Samuel 12:1–7

Rhetoric is the art of igniting language. Many people are suspicious of it. However, just because techniques can be used to corrupt and distort, it does not mean that the techniques are wrong in themselves. Through the carefully crafted words of Nathan the prophet, God speaks. Rhetorical devices are used to get under the wire of David's defences, after his acts of adultery and murder (2 Samuel 11).

The features of the parable are drawn from a world with which David is familiar. It is woven around the narrative staple of a rich man and a poor man, a memorable and therefore common feature of oral discourse. There is an incremental use of pathos, the layering up of words and images designed to provoke emotional response.

The rich man with his '*very many* flocks and herds' (v. 2) is contrasted with the poor man who had 'nothing but one little ewe lamb' (v. 3). The pathos builds as we read that the lamb has been brought up with the poor man's children, sharing his 'meagre fare'. This lamb, nursed like a child, becomes like a daughter to him (v. 3).

The introduction of the traveller presents the need to provide hospitality. The rich man's meanness is emphasised as we recall that with his 'very many flocks' he has ample resources for his guest. The narrative trap is sprung as the wealthy man helps himself to the poor man's lamb. In a moment of dramatic irony, David erupts in a rage that will shift to penitence as Nathan's bald statement 'You are the man!' (v. 7) hits home. Had Nathan baldly accused David, he would have met with a defensive, even aggressive response. Nathan's storytelling approach means that David is able to recognise his sin.

God speaks through language. In the teaching of Jesus we see language used powerfully in imagery, analogy, parable, metaphor and aphorism. Leaders and preachers need to learn the art of persuasion. Boring preaching in God's name is a form of heresy, as it suggests that God is dull and uninspiring. Rhetoric is theologically important, and not a dirty word.

5 God communicates in practical care

1 Kings 19:4–16

Elijah is a broken man. The triumphs of his encounter with the prophets of Baal in chapter 18 have been snuffed out by terror and exhaustion. He sits in the wilderness under a solitary broom tree, praying to die (v. 4). How does God communicate in Elijah's night-time of fear?

Unexpected and unbidden, the messenger of God is in the heart of the situation (v. 5b). Before words are spoken, the angel touches Elijah and encourages him to get up and eat what has been prepared for him, and to drink water. The presence of God in the heart of Elijah's misery is marked by practical care and a striking lack of words.

The first thing the angel does is to touch Elijah. There is something simple, compassionate and moving in this act of communication. Elijah is given rest and sustenance (v. 7). It is only because he has received such care that Elijah is able to travel the distance necessary for him to arrive at a place of profound encounter, where he is able to articulate his anguish (v. 10), discern God's presence in the 'sound of sheer silence' (v. 12), and hear God's calling afresh (vv. 13–18).

In the raising of Jairus' daughter, we are offered the little detail that Jesus 'took her by the hand' (Mark 5:41; Matthew 9:25) before she got up. This physical contact is an aspect of the healing. It summons the girl back to herself. In Mark's account, the command '*Talitha cum*', meaning 'Little girl, get up!' comes after the touch. In Matthew's account there are no words accompanying the miracle; touch alone brings her back.

Touch—used wisely, compassionately and appropriately, orientated towards the needs of the other—is perhaps the greatest gift of solace any of us can offer or receive. Tragically, in our over-sexualised culture, many are afraid of this gift, either because it has been misused in the past or because they fear it will be misinterpreted. Nevertheless, offered wisely, compassionately and appropriately, it opens up a field of communication when words are futile. The divine voice can speak wordlessly through human touch and practical care.

6 God of white-hot holiness

It is wise to remember that God is 'other', dwelling in white-hot holiness from which, in his mercy, he comes to us veiled. Isaiah 6 offers a glimpse of this holiness as the earthly temple and heavenly courts elide in an awesome, overwhelming vision. The divine holiness highlights Isaiah's uncleanliness and that of his people, which leads him to profound despair (v. 5).

The vision is full of sensory communication from one who transcends earthly dimensions such that the 'hem of his robe filled the temple' (v. 1). Isaiah sees the Lord enthroned, with seraphs in attendance highlighting his otherness. We can almost hear the sound of their beating wings. The senses are overwhelmed as the angelic voices cause the 'pivots on the thresholds' to shake and smoke billows through the space (v. 4). The cleansing of the prophet comes as a form of cauterisation, as a live coal is applied to his lips, 'blotting out' his sin (v. 7). It is an overpowering revelation of God's holiness.

This otherness is revealed to Peter, James and John in the momentous mystery of the transfiguration. Here too was sensory overload as Jesus' 'face shone like the sun, and his clothes became dazzling white' (Matthew 17:2), while mysterious figures resembling Moses and Elijah came into view. The otherness is underscored by the overshadowing 'bright cloud' and the disembodied voice naming Jesus' identity, delighting in him and calling the disciples to 'listen to him' (v. 5). Like Isaiah in the temple, the disciples on the mountaintop are 'overcome by fear' (v. 6). Isaiah's fear lies in his recognition of sin, which is resolved by the cauterisation. The disciples' fear is quelled by the reassuring touch of Jesus and his instruction, 'Get up and do not be afraid' (v. 7).

In the transfiguration we see divine communication expressed in transcendence and immanence, the holiness of God communicated through strange event and intimate touch. We need to hold the two in tension. If we focus too much on God's immanence, there is a danger that we might believe we can manipulate the divine to our own ends, making God in our own image. If we focus too much on God's otherness, we forget his tenderness.

Guidelines

- Jacob so desires God's blessing that he will not let go of his divine opponent. What does God's blessing mean to you?
- God enables those he calls. Spiritual writers have called this 'the grace of office'. Pray for those in senior leadership in church and state, that they might know this grace.
- Pray for all who visit holy spaces today, that they will experience God through the buildings. If you have artistic gifts, how could you put them to God's service?
- If you are a preacher, pray for skill in working with words that reveal the Word. Commit to learning more about the art of preaching. (See the further reading list.)
- Pray for people who have been damaged by inappropriate touch. How might you employ touch wisely to communicate love and reassurance?
- Do the songs you use in your church hold in tension divine immanence and transcendence, or do they favour one theological perspective over the other?

1 God who speaks through angels

Genesis 16:7–16; Luke2:8–20

Throughout the Bible, angels warn, direct and comfort in the name of God. These messengers are an essential arm of the divine communications team. The 'angel of the Lord' is mentioned 58 times in the Old Testament, representing God in human form, usually appearing in times of dire need, bringing news of salvation.

In Genesis 16 we focus on Hagar, Sarai's maidservant. She has been given to Abram by Sarai in the hope that, through her, Abram would have a child (vv. 1–6). Having conceived, Hagar foolishly regards her barren mistress with contempt. Sarai, consumed with jealousy, treats Hagar terribly. Rather than offering the mother of his unborn child protection, Abram abdicates responsibility, so Hagar flees into the wilderness, pregnant without provision or protection. Into this dire situation steps the angel of the Lord; God communicates in the midst of messy human relationships.

His word is challenging and full of promise. The challenge is to return to Sarai and submit; perhaps the divine word is to 'drop the attitude'. The staggering promise is that she will be included alongside Abram in the prophecy of countless descendants. Abram is the great patriarch, she a powerless slave woman, and yet her children will be a multitude beyond number (v. 10). Her son, Ishmael, will live the life of a Bedouin—a life of freedom at the margins—and it seems that he will inherit his mother's gift for conflicted relationships (v. 12; see Genesis 16:5)! Towards the end of the encounter, Hagar realises that she has been conversing with 'El-roi', the God who sees (v. 13). It is clear that God continues to watch over Hagar and Ishmael, as the angel of the Lord intervenes again later, when they find themselves banished, out of resources and facing death (21:15–19).

Angels have a habit of dealing with marginal characters. In Luke 2 we see the astonishing revelation of the birth of Jesus to uneducated men with no social standing. These shepherds are on the receiving end of the full angelic line-up: the angel of the Lord is surrounded by the heavenly host in full chorus. The work of angels points us to the God who lifts up the lowly. It begs the question, where does the church step out with such angelic intent?

2 God who speaks to 'outsiders'

Matthew 2:1–12

It is clear that the magi from the east were Gentiles, probably astrologers, and most definitely outsiders to the concerns of Israel. Yet they recognised the strange star as a sign, connected to the child to be born king of the Jews. Ironically, it is the outsiders who are drawn to this birth, who 'come to pay him homage'. Having observed 'his star' (v. 2), they travel miles, bringing gifts fit for a king (v. 11). In contrast, the religious elite, assembled by a frightened Herod (v. 3), are able to recall prophetic words but don't act on them. God reaches out to the astrologers in a language they understand—through the stars. In response, the magi go and search for the child. God reaches out to his own people through the language of the prophets, but the religious leaders don't appear to express much interest in response.

Do we ever assume that God is 'for us' but not 'for them'? Do we think we have God all taped up? Has smug complacency smothered all expectation? The presence of these Gentile astrologers, kneeling before the Christ, tells us loud and clear: no one can claim a monopoly on God.

God's communicative zeal shatters expectations. As Jesus reminded the townspeople of Nazareth (Luke 4:25–27), Elijah wasn't sent to the widows of Israel, but to the poor Gentile widow of Zarephath (1 Kings 17:9–16); Elisha didn't heal the lepers of Israel, but a rich Gentile commander, Na'aman of Syria (2 Kings 5:1–14). God makes 'outsiders' into 'insiders' and crosses over the boundaries of our limited expectation.

So often we draw lines between those we identify as 'goodies', the 'in group', and those 'baddies' over there. What underlies our need to label, demarcate, separate and divide? Fear, insecurity, the need for control and power, pride, lack of forgiveness or understanding, resentment… to name just a few.

Young children do it: '*You* can play our game; *you* can't.' Families do it: 'We don't talk to Uncle So-and-so.' Nations do it: 'God is on our side.' The church does it—different groups drawing lines and claiming that God is with them and against others.

See the astrologers kneeling before the Christ-child: God just doesn't play by our 'insider/ outsider' rules.

3 God speaks in skin

John 1:1–18

John's prologue is a masterful exploration of the nature and identity of the Word who 'became flesh and lived among us' (v. 14). John begins by echoing the opening to the book of Genesis: 'In the beginning…'. He draws from Wisdom tradition to paint a picture of Jesus as God's agent in creation. Through the incarnation, this pre-existent Word is embodied in flesh in the person of Jesus Christ—God's ultimate speech-act. It is Christ who makes the Father known. In Christ, God speaks in skin.

For many people in our society, God seems a distant irrelevancy. One Facebook acquaintance of mine calls him the 'sky fairy'. Mythic, fantasy, mere human projection… God doesn't get a great press in some quarters. Yet, serious reflection on the accounts of Jesus' life points us to the God who communicates in skin, as Jesus teaches, heals, challenges, subverts, and welcomes undesirables. His light, shining in the darkness, highlights the shadows around him—love throwing evil into relief. Human authorities are threatened by the power of this vulnerability, and so they abuse him and nail him up. In resurrection light, God again speaks in skin—scarred skin, which proclaims that love can never be defeated and that death will not have the final word. 'The light shines in the darkness, and the darkness did not overcome it.' (v. 5).

The incarnation is, at heart, a message of the most profound hope, a message of grace and truth. In a world of fear, war, terrorism and despondency, God is not distant and uninterested, but is intimately involved in human experience. Jesus knows the reality of our humanity and is able to 'sympathise with our weaknesses' (Hebrews 4:15).

In Christ we are shown the nature of God and are called to work with God, that he might speak through our own frail humanity. God spoke ultimately in skin in Christ; he still speaks in skin through his people. The hand that reaches out, the arms that encircle, the eyes that weep, the face that smiles, the mouth that speaks words of encouragement can all put flesh on the communication of God in the here and now. God still speaks in our vulnerable human skin.

4 God captures imaginations

Luke 15:8–10

Jesus used the currency of the ordinary—mustard seeds, pearls, rich men and debtors, lost sheep, houses built on sand and rock—to invite the eye of the hearer's imagination to open upon vistas of new possibility.

The parable of the lost coin is a compact endorsement of the role of the imagination in conveying spiritual truth. In this particular parable, Jesus uses the currency, quite literally, of his day to capture the imagination of his hearers. They would have known the terrible anxiety caused by the loss of such a coin. In this vignette God is painted as a woman, desperately seeking something precious. Can you feel her rising panic as she sweeps and seeks?

Imagine you are due to leave for the airport and you can't locate your passport. You tear the house apart looking for it. Feel that sense of panic and urgency. 'Where did I put it?' Now feel the adrenaline subside as you find it in that secure place where no burglar would ever think to look.

Let's up the stakes. You're on the beach; your child is playing by the water's edge, busily engaged in sandcastle building. You glance away, look back, and can't locate them. You scan the shoreline. Nothing. You run closer, your eyes roving wildly, heart starting to thump, thump, thump. Imagine the relief and joy when you see your child pootling along in the shallows.

This is the urgency with which the woman seeks her coin. This is the urgency with which we are called to search for those who have lost their way—because this is the urgency with which God looks for his beloved, you and me, and all those people who struggle on and have no idea that they are profoundly loved and valued by their Creator.

Our human propensity to shortsightedness is breathtaking. Without the discipline of allowing God to heal our foresight and insight, we quickly revert to selfishness, narrow perspective and self-delusion. God calls us to have our imaginations reshaped by his love, so that we see with his vision and speak with his passion. Conversion is, at heart, the reorientating of the imagination. Growth in the life of faith involves the daily act of reenvisioning the world in the light of God's sacrificial love.

5 God speaks from darkness into darkness

Mark 15:33–39; Psalm 22

On the cross, at the darkest moment metaphorically and actually, Jesus echoes the opening of Psalm 22: 'My God, my God, why have you forsaken me?' In what sense can we speak of God's presence in the darkness of the cross? Much depends on how we understand the person of Jesus. If he is the Word made flesh, then the cry from the cross expresses a divine experience of utter abandonment. Pain, the weight of evil, darkness and isolation surround Jesus such that he feels utterly separated from the love of God. The crucifixion stabs the unity of the Trinity. This is a powerful reminder to the human sufferer that the experience of human anguish is not unknown to God. God speaks from darkness into our darkest situations.

We can read the cry from the cross as an expression of desperation and as an act of trust, a crying out in the hope of being heard. Certainly this is the purpose of Psalm 22, which weaves together potent themes of lament, calling to God from a place of profound suffering (vv. 1–2, 6–8, 11–18), and powerful themes of praise (vv. 3–5, 9–10, 19–21a). The psalm moves through lament and ends on notes of praise and thanksgiving (vv. 21b–31).

Given that Jesus would have been familiar with the whole psalm, it is possible to see, in his recitation of the first verse, that he is opening himself to the hope embedded in the rest of the psalm, seeking the presence of God in the words of the psalmist. Perhaps this claim is tenuous, but the human experience of seeking God and hearing God in the midst of despair and suffering is often tenuous—a groping towards light from a place where faith is in danger of being snuffed out.

Deep in the dark heart of Auschwitz, in the cell in the prison where Father Maximilian Kolbe died, having swapped places with a prisoner sentenced to death, there burns a paschal candle. Night and day this light shines out, speaking of the greater light that cannot be overcome. The constant flame speaks of God's presence in acts of courage, miserable suffering and raw injustice. Those who perpetrated that evil are long gone, but the light shines on, speaking from the darkness into the darkness, and pointing to redemptive hope.

6 God of the dawning light

John 20:1–18

'Early on the first day of the week, while it was still dark, Mary Magdalene came to the tomb' (John 20:1). The language points us towards the darkness of Mary's despairing grief, and yet the hint of hope is there. The first day of the week is the first day of something new.

Mary grasps at the most natural human explanation for the empty tomb—grave robbery. The light has not yet dawned (vv. 2, 13, 15). After Peter and the other disciple have left the scene, Mary is alone, weeping (v. 11). In spite of encountering two angels in white who question the reason for her tears, the light has not yet breached the clouds of her confusion. When she turns and sees Jesus standing behind her, she fits his appearance into her preexistent framework of assumptions. It's a garden; he must be a gardener (v. 15). How often do we miss seeing God at work because of our assumptions?

There is a delicious irony about this case of mistaken identity, given the many biblical references to God as the gardener. You're right, Mary, in thinking he's a gardener; you just don't yet know how right you are. The truth eventually dawns on her when Jesus speaks her name, and her eyes are opened: 'Mary!' … 'Rabbouni!' (v. 16). The sunlight pierces the clouds and she declares, 'I have seen the Lord' (v. 18).

We see a similar theme in the beautiful imagery of the Benedictus: 'By the tender mercy of our God, the dawn from on high will break upon us, to give light to those who sit in darkness and in the shadow of death, to guide our feet into the way of peace' (Luke 1:78–79).

When night falls in our lives, in the shape of death, despair, depression or any of the myriad miseries of human life, how can we be sure that the light will dawn? When we are in the shadows, we cannot always hold on to hope for ourselves. We need others to remind us that God is the God of dawning light. When others are in such places, we need to hold the light for them, confident that because the dawn from on high broke in with resurrection glory, the dawn will always break, no matter how dark the night.

Nothing eclipses the communicative power of God!

Guidelines

- Angels are often found in the Bible with the outsider, ministering in dire situations. Do an inventory of the active angelic intent of your church. Consider the theme of 'insiders/outsiders'. Are there particular people or groups you know, that you don't pray for because they are 'beyond the pale', for personal or political reasons? Take time to name them in your prayers.
- Are there people in your life who regard God as little more than a 'sky fairy'? Pray that they will encounter the risen Christ in ways that cannot be explained away and ignored. Pray for God's blessing upon them.
- Pray for a release of imagination in the church's communication in all contexts—through art and performance; in preaching, to engage and draw in, to teach, challenge, reorientate and encourage.
- Pray for Christians working in the media and the arts—for example, Springs Dance Company, Riding Lights, and all Christian dancers, performers and comedians.
- Take time to bring to God your view of a difficult situation, perhaps at work or in your personal life. Talk to him about how you see things. Name any frustration, anger or hurt. Now ask him to open the eyes of your imagination to new perspectives and possibilities.
- Pray for those who are in the experience of deep anguish, that the dawn from on high might break upon them.
- Pray for those you know for whom faith is beginning to dawn, that they might meet the risen Christ.
- Reflecting on the themes of the last two weeks, draw up a list of the ways you experience the communicative power of God.

FURTHER READING

K. Bruce, *Igniting the Heart: Preaching and imagination*, SCM, 2015.

M. Forsythe, *The Elements of Eloquence: How to turn the perfect English phrase*, Icon, 2014.

S. Leith, *'You Talkin' to Me?' Rhetoric from Aristotle to Obama*, Profile, 2012.

Haggai and Joel

Haggai and Joel were probably both post-exilic prophets, but separated by more than half a century. They addressed the people of Judah at times when local agriculture was undergoing crisis, claiming that the root cause lay in the people's relationship to God. Unlike prophets of the pre-exilic period, neither Haggai nor Joel pointed to social injustice as the people's spiritual problem, but held that the heart of the issue was the temple and the worship offered there. This has led commentators to surmise that both prophets may have been either priests or cultic prophets (whose normal function may have been to lead worshippers in the temple in supplication, and then to supply oracular reassurance that sincere prayer would be answered).

Towards the end of both Haggai and Joel's books, the focus on responding to the agricultural crisis through turning to God in the temple gives way to more far-reaching prophecies about the centrality of Jerusalem in God's ultimate purposes. The writing therefore takes on eschatological or apocalyptic qualities.

The dates of Haggai's prophecies are very clear, since they are given in the text. He addressed the people between August and December of 520BC (the second year of Darius I of Persia). He was contemporaneous with Zechariah, who, like him, called for the rebuilding of the partially ruined temple, although Zechariah's prophecies continued two years after Haggai's ceased.

Ideas about Joel's dates have varied widely, ranging from the eighth century BC (before the exile) to the fourth century BC. Most contemporary scholars, however, place him in the second half of the fifth century, after the periods of Haggai and Zechariah, Ezra and Nehemiah, when the temple had been rebuilt and Jerusalem restored but Judah remained part of the Persian empire.

Quotations are taken from the New Revised Standard Version.

1 Wrong priorities

Haggai 1:1–11

First we meet 'the prophet' Haggai (vv. 1, 3). This description may mean that he was a cultic prophet (see Introduction), but it certainly means that through him the word of the Lord came with messages for his time. His oracles expressed neither his own generalised critique of the situation in Judah nor his vague aspirations for its future. His words were accepted as messages from God for that time. The first message was on 'the first day of the month' (v. 1), the new moon festival, when the people gathered to make a burnt offering. The dilapidated state of the temple would have been very obvious to them.

Second, we meet Zerubbabel, who, despite having a Babylonian name, was of David's lineage. He had returned from Babylon under the authority of the Persian emperor, Darius I (reigned 522–486BC). Zerubbabel is described as 'governor', although it is unclear whether this means that Judah was treated as a separate province by the Persians at this time or was merely a sub-province under Samaria. Third, we meet Joshua, 'the high priest', the first so described in Jerusalem after the exile. Like Zerubbabel, he had come from Babylon with authority to rebuild the temple, which had been burnt down by the Babylonians in 586BC.

A previous attempt to restore the temple had been stopped largely through conflict with higher provincial authorities in Samaria (see Ezra 4). Haggai's first messages to the leaders and people of his day challenge them to take up the task again. The oracles baldly make a link between their procrastination and the agricultural and economic slump they are suffering. Far from being a reason to put off the task further, drought is the Lord's chastisement for wrong priorities (vv. 10–11).

It is understandable that, after returning from exile, people might prioritise house-building (though their houses may not have been 'panelled', as NRSV translates verse 4, but just 'roofed'). But it seems clear that the temple, although it had been used for worship by those left in the land while others were taken into exile, was a roofless shell. Haggai's message bursts in as a call to give priority to rebuilding *God's* house, expecting that this will be the route to an abundance that has so far eluded the people.

2 'Take courage'

Haggai 1:12—2:9

Oracles of chastisement give way swiftly to words of encouragement. At the first signs of obedience from leaders and people, Haggai's message is, 'I am with you, says the Lord' (1:13).

Rebuilding a ruined temple would take time. First there was the wood to be fetched from Judah's hills (forested at that time), as the Lord commanded (1:8); then rubble needed to be cleared and the displaced stones of the broken building reassembled. Maybe, too, there were beams of Lebanese cedar, left behind when the previous restoration project was halted (Ezra 3:7), to be manoeuvred laboriously into position, ready to make roofs and walls—and all this by people malnourished during the drought. No wonder, then, that seven weeks after his original prophesying, Haggai and the people, looking round, are disappointed that little has yet been achieved (2:3). Nevertheless, his message remains encouraging: three times he says, 'Take courage' (literally, 'Be strong')—to governor, priest and people (v. 4).

This encouragement is rooted not just in God's response to human obedience, but in his abiding promise, going back to the original exodus from Egypt (vv. 4–5). It is in God's faithfulness rather than our own that his people's confidence should always rest. God promises to be with his people, and here it is expressed explicitly in terms of his spirit's presence. In Exodus 35:30–35, the divine spirit is shown particularly in the skills of craftsmen working on the tent of meeting. The same idea may be present here, but with a wider meaning, underlining that the Lord has never really been absent and will once again make Jerusalem his home, and that the people's worship in the temple will not be in vain.

Next comes a surprising promise, looking into the future (although a future said to be not far off), when God will 'shake' the heavens, the earth and all nations, to bring into the renewed temple the treasures of all the world (vv. 6–9). Perhaps this prophecy was given when the provincial authorities in Samaria were commanded to support the temple out of royal revenues (see Ezra 6:8–12), which would have encouraged Haggai. Nevertheless, the scope of his prophecy leaps from the realm of the historical into the realm of eschatology—God's great day to come.

3 'From this day on…'

Two more months have passed, and it seems that Haggai's prophecy is slipping back to its original theme. He asks the priests to reflect on the hard times the nation has been going through (v. 16), in terms reminiscent of 1:9. But the prophecy goes on, 'I struck you and all the products of your toil with blight and mildew and hail; yet you did not return to me, says the Lord' (v. 17). Here, drought is not mentioned. Apparently there have been new setbacks to their farming and food supply.

This dialogue with the priests is an invitation to reflect, framed in questions which ask them to give a ruling about whether holiness is contagious in ritual terms (vv. 11–12) and whether impurity is contaminating (v. 13). Unfortunately the answer to the first question is 'no', but to the second, 'yes'. Haggai uses this understanding of ritual purity as a parable about the nation and its worship. There was something that contaminated their worship: maybe it was complacency; maybe it was the desecrated nature of the unrestored temple itself. Nevertheless, these sombre reflections can give way before sheer grace, because the message continues, 'From this day on I will bless you' (v. 19).

What is the significance of 'this day'? Some commentators believe that this dialogue between Haggai and the priests took place on the day of a ceremony to 'refound' the temple, maybe the day on which positive construction began. It is unlikely that it would have involved the laying of foundation stones in the lowest course of the building, since the continuance of the temple as a place of worship during the exile suggests that the lower courses of the walls had not been brought right down to the ground in 586BC. Nevertheless, 'this day' was a turning point because, in some sense, 'the foundation of the Lord's temple' was being laid (v. 18). It occurred in December, when the new seed would have just been sown after the autumn rains, so Haggai was prophesying abundance for the future at the agricultural turning point of the year. There is a very similar prophecy in Zechariah 8:9–13 about the laying of a foundation for the rebuilding of the temple, from which point blessings would flow once more to the people.

4 'On that day...'

Haggai 2:20–23

Haggai's final oracles move from 'this day' to 'that day'—the 'Day of the Lord', when the Davidic kingdom will be reestablished in Judah, and God will triumph over all the other nations of the earth. Once more he speaks about the Lord shaking the earth, and he follows with a description of 'holy war', similar to many other eschatological and apocalyptic passages in the Old Testament.

Haggai seems to have believed that all this would happen in the very near future. Like the previous ones, these oracles were also uttered on the day when the temple was 'refounded', with Zerubbabel, the Davidic heir, taking a key role. Not long before this date, the throne of the Persian King Darius had been challenged severely by unrest, and, although Darius had retrieved the situation, a vivid impression that he was not invulnerable must have remained in his subjects' minds. In these circumstances, Haggai could imagine that the refounding of the temple marked a major turning-point in world history, and could believe that the glorious future for Judah and Jerusalem foreseen by earlier prophets was about to break in.

Although Haggai does not explicitly call Zerubbabel a king, the implication is unmistakable in his words. Verse 23 describes Zerubbabel as God's 'servant', like David (see 1 Kings 11:34; Psalm 78:70; Ezekiel 34:23). The curse uttered against his grandfather Jeconiah in Jeremiah 22:24–25 (there identified by his other name, Jehoiachin) is reversed, as the Lord makes Zerubbabel his 'signet ring', signifying that he will always be with the Lord and that through him God's authority will be attested to the people. This is a messianic picture. However, it was not fulfilled in the person of Zerubbabel, who disappears from historical records soon after this date.

Whatever Zerubbabel's fate, the messianic hope remained alive in the Jewish people, and his memory continues to be honoured as one of those through whom the Lord delivered his people. A well-known Hanukkah hymn says, 'Well nigh had I perished when Babylon's end drew near; through Zerubbabel was I saved after seventy years.' Haggai's prophecies are part of a long direction of travel in Jewish thought, even if his predictions were not historically precise.

5 'Has such a thing happened...?'

We turn now to the prophet Joel. During a terrible catastrophe, people understandably see their experience as unique in history. This seems to have been Joel's sense when Judah experienced a devastating locust invasion, accompanied by a severe period of scorching drought that caused brush fires. His opening lament asks if any such disaster has ever happened before, and recommends that it be recorded for posterity (vv. 2–3), inverting the more usual command in the Hebrew scriptures to remember and recall God's saving acts of mercy. Unfortunately for those trying to work out Joel's dates, these particular events were not recorded in any other surviving annals, and his words stand alone as their record.

Some commentators see Joel's prophecies about locusts as figurative; they think that he was really prophesying about an invading army. Others say that his prophecy begins with a literal locust infestation in chapter 1, but, by chapter 2, is predicting a foreign invasion. However, I believe that throughout his work, Joel is describing agricultural disasters that the people were currently experiencing. He uses all the artistry of a poet to underline the tragedy and employs increasingly heightened language as his oracles progress. Even here in chapter 1, the rhetorical use of four different terms for locusts in verse 4 (the cutter, the hopper, the swarmer and the destroyer) conveys dramatically the inexorable advance of these insects over the land and all its vegetation, and the utter devastation they wreak.

What should be the human response to such catastrophe? For Joel, it is that people should wake up, lament, be dismayed and wail, turning to ritual prayer in the temple with fasting and the wearing of sackcloth, which signified both grief and penitence. We might nowadays talk about 'ceasing to be in denial'. It is perhaps no coincidence that Joel's first clarion call is to drunkards (v. 5), since inebriation is so often a route that people choose to blot out reality. But they chase a fool's paradise in their drunkenness, since the nation's disaster directly affects the source of the wine on which they rely (vv. 5, 7).

Joel does not specify the nation's sin in his calls to lament, but by implication it looks as though complacency is an important part of the problem.

6 National lamentation

Joel was very familiar with temple rituals (see the Introduction). For him, the fact that the disaster made the daily offerings impossible (v. 9) shows the spiritual depth of the nation's crisis. These offerings were the conditions for God's meeting with his people (Exodus 29:42–43) and were very important to the post-exilic community: an earlier governor and his colleagues had made a costly pledge to perpetuate them (Nehemiah 10:32–33). So the priests would have had good reason to mourn, both for religious reasons and for personal ones, since they had a share in the offerings for their own use. Joel exhorts them to use their loss as the motivation to call a day of national mourning, a 'solemn assembly' of fasting and prayer in the temple (vv. 13–14).

Repeatedly Joel describes the destruction of agricultural produce (vv. 9, 12, 17). Speaking poetically of withered joy (v. 12) and departed gladness (v. 16), he spells out the human consequences of the disaster, especially how worship has changed from gladness to lamentation. Verse 19 is one of several occasions when Joel seems to propose the words that people might use in their prayer.

Joel also depicts other parts of creation feeling dismay: in verse 10 the ground itself mourns, and in verses 18 and 20 he speaks of the grief and prayer of animals. He expresses a real sense of the solidarity between different parts of creation, which perhaps we need to reappropriate.

All this vivid description points to a disturbing conclusion—that 'the day of the Lord is near' and that it comes 'as destruction from the Almighty' (v. 15). Amos had already declared that the 'day of the Lord' was for judgement, not blessing on God's people (Amos 5:18–20). Joel and other subsequent prophets followed Amos' line of thought—but is it '*the* day of the Lord' (the final judgement) or '*a* day of the Lord' (an interim one) that Joel foresees? It is not clear. By the end of the book, the phrase ' day of the Lord' has taken on a distinctively eschatological meaning, signifying the day of judgement on Israel's enemies.

Guidelines

One commentator sums up Haggai's work in this way:

Whilst his predictions were not fulfilled in any literal way, Haggai's prophecy was effective. He achieved what he set out to do, to have the temple rebuilt. The rebuilding of the temple was beneficial to the Jewish community, even if the conditions of life were not radically transformed... Of course, there is no reason to doubt that Haggai was sincere in his predictions and that he expected that a glorious future was at hand. Utopian dreams, however, have proven fickle for many prophets and visionaries besides Haggai. The strength of such visions is that they inspire hope and empower people to act in difficult situations. The danger, however, is that disillusionment may set in when the glorious promises are not fulfilled.

John J. Collins, *Joel, Obadiah, Haggai, Zechariah, Malachi*

Can you think of modern 'prophecies' that have worked to energise people and create change for good? Take the opportunity to thank God for them.

What helps people sustain hope and follow the direction of travel that might lead to its fulfilment, when they are disappointed in the short term? Pray for the sustaining of Godly hope in this world.

How far can Christians embrace the following words of Václav Havel about hope?

Hope is not a prognostication –it's an orientation of the spirit… Hope is definitely NOT the same as optimism. It's not the conviction that something will turn out well, but the certainty that something makes sense, regardless of how it turns out.

Disturbing the Peace (Vintage, 1991), ch. 5

1 'Blow the trumpet'

Joel 2:1–11

Twice in chapter 2, Joel calls the people to 'blow the trumpet in Zion' (vv. 1, 15). This is the ram's horn, the *shophar*, used by the Israelites in war (see

Joshua 6:4–20), to assemble the people (Numbers 29:1) and in worship (Psalm 150:3). Here in Joel 2, the first call is to warn of an invading army. It seems that the people's troubles are about to get worse—the (or 'a') 'day of the Lord is coming' (v. 1), and it will be unendurable (v. 11). Later, the trumpet will be blown to call the people together in response (2:15).

Although some commentators have seen the 'great and powerful army' in verse 2 as humans, in verse 7 they are *compared* to warriors and soldiers rather than identified with them. I think it best to see this as a renewed prophecy about locusts. The strongest argument for the 'human' view is based on a later part of this chapter, where the invaders are described as 'the northern army' (2:20). Locust swarms affecting the Holy Land typically originate from the south, in Egypt or Sudan. However, in the period of the prophets the north was particularly associated with danger and invasion, and the words 'the northern army' are perhaps being used symbolically to denote threat. Alternatively, it may be that the swarm is predicted to come (atypically) from Persia.

A swarm of locusts darkens the sky for many (sometimes hundreds) of square miles and moves like an irresistible invader. Perhaps the fires mentioned in verse 3 are kindled by people in vain attempts to break the swarm's advance. Thick smoke would increase the obscuring of sun, moon and stars (v. 10). In their flight, locusts make a powerful noise—compared by some to waves of rain, but here to 'the crackling of a flame' (v. 5). The prophet's words about darkness and fire, together with words about the earth quaking (v. 10), make this prophecy tremble between a vivid description of natural disaster and a sense that the 'last things' are in play. The most terrifying aspect is that it is 'the Lord' who commands and leads this army (v. 11), which is why this is 'the' or 'a' day of the Lord, and a sign that the people are under judgement.

2 'Rend your hearts and not your clothing'

Joel 2:12–17

Despite the extreme crisis that the prophet sees, it is still a time of choice (as the word 'crisis' really implies—coming from a Greek word meaning 'decision'). There remains room for a return to the Lord, and the invitation to do so, introduced by the phrase 'Yet even now' (v. 12), comes from his own mouth, even though the previous verse depicts him as the triumphantly shouting head of the locust army. The reminder of God's constant graciousness and mercy (v. 13), in words also found elsewhere in the Old Testament (Exodus 34:6; Psalm 86:5; Jonah 4:2), points to the real possibility that national penitence will avert total calamity. The 'Who knows…?' of verse 14 expresses poignant hope in the underlying nature of this merciful God and his covenant with his people.

The call to 'rend your hearts and not your clothing' (v. 13) asks for inward sincerity rather than outward ritual, and may remind Christian readers of Paul's use of the idea of the true circumcision 'of the heart' (Romans 2:29). However, it is clear that Joel does not believe that inward sincerity *replaces* outward ritual, for the second call of the trumpet is for a religious assembly in the temple, involving everyone (v. 16). Once again, Joel supplies words for the people's prayer (v. 17)—words appealing to God's concern for his reputation among the nations, a reputation that is bound up with his people's welfare. This is a theme found also in Deuteronomy 9:26–29, Isaiah 37:20 and Ezekiel 36:20–21.

Much of the apocalyptic imagery used by Joel reappears and is reused in the New Testament. Some Christians, when they think about the 'last things', interpret the imagery almost fatalistically, as if 'these things are bound to happen'. Yet we should remember that embedded in the thought of coming judgement is the hope expressed in the phrases 'Yet even now…' and 'Who knows…?'

3 God's jealousy and mercy

Joel 2:18–29

Suddenly the tone changes, as well as the tense. So vividly does Joel prophesy a reversal in God's treatment of his people that he speaks of it as having been already achieved (v. 18). As we read on in the passage, we find this 'predictive past tense' interspersed with a future tense (as in vv. 20, 24–27). The people's return to prayer and devotion will more than reverse the disasters they have suffered. They will no longer be a mockery among the nations (v. 19): their 'reminder' to God of the danger of this outcome will have effectively provoked him to jealousy for his name, so that he will have acted on their behalf.

This concept of God's jealousy—his desire to maintain his reputation among the nations—seems at first glance to be a very human one, yet it is deeply bound up with the mystery of Israel's election. It is what the Lord does among his chosen people which will, in the end, call the other nations to him (as in Isaiah 2:2–4). However, in the context of today's passage we should also notice that it is not only God's shame that is done away with when he restores his people, but theirs too (vv. 25–26). God is motivated not only by jealousy but also by his mercy towards them, which is not limited but is overflowing (v. 24). And, as the people are blessed, so too the natural world receives the divine word to it: 'Do not fear' (vv. 21–22).

In oracles of great poetic force we read that the locusts will be scattered to the east, with many perishing on the shores of the Dead Sea, and to the west, where they will fall beside the Mediterranean. The rains will fall; the crops will abound. Like Second Isaiah, Joel dares to see God's blessing as a 'repayment' (v. 25; Isaiah 40:10) or recompense for what the people have suffered. As Christians, too, we believe that God has already shown mercy, in Jesus, and proclaimed the 'just reward' for his obedient suffering; we are given the opportunity to appropriate this recompense and experience its results. Do we believe as vividly as Joel that the state of grace to which we are called will also bring healing to the land and the rest of the animal kingdom?

4 Signs of the Day of the Lord

Joel 2:26–32

Twice Joel prophesies 'never again' (vv. 26–27), raising these oracles of blessing to the level of 'end-times' prophecy. It was believed from the time of the tabernacle, which was carried by the wandering people of the exodus (Exodus 25:8–9, 14), that the presence of the Lord was 'in the midst of Israel ' (Joel 2:27). This idea had regained fresh importance for the post-exilic prophets, with their focus upon the rebuilt temple; allied to the conviction of monotheism, which the exile had clarified for them, it is a powerful idea. But here, Joel's words take the picture to a more surprising level yet: God's presence 'in the midst' will be evidenced in the availability of the divine spirit to all God's people, not just to prophets (vv. 28–29). A new era of spiritual gifts will be the evidence of the 'new covenant' prophesied by Jeremiah (Jeremiah 31:31–34).

In verse 30 we move from oracular poetry to prophecy in prose, describing 'the great and terrible day of the Lord', accompanied by portents in the heavens and upon earth. This passage probably did not originate 'of a piece' with the two preceding verses, yet their position side by side in the finished book of Joel has indelibly linked them as a description of different aspects of the 'end times', the human and the cosmic. Christians are probably most familiar with verses 28–32 as they are used in Peter's speech in Acts 2:17–21), in which he explains the meaning of the phenomena experienced at the first Christian Pentecost. By using this passage of Joel, Peter's speech highlights a link between the outpouring of the Spirit of prophecy on the disciples, so that they come to proclaim the mighty acts of God in different languages, and the cosmic phenomenon of fire, which they experience as 'tongues, as of fire' coming to rest on each of them (Acts 2:2–3). All this meant that the event of Pentecost was a sign of the coming 'day of the Lord' (described by Joel as 'terrible' but in Acts 20:20 as 'glorious'). Both Joel and Acts emphasise both the salvation destined for 'everyone who calls upon the name of the Lord' (Joel 2:32; Acts 2:21) and the divine initiative in this salvation, in that it is the Lord who calls them (Joel 2:32; Acts 2:39).

5 Neighbouring nations reap their just deserts

Joel 3:1–8

We continue with prophecy in prose; we have already left behind the crisis of the locust invasion, which occupies most of the book of Joel, and it may be that the later prophecies in the book come from a different time and a different voice. Although we cannot date them (just as we cannot date Joel's prophecies about the locust invasion), they concern recognisable historical realities that the Israelites experienced over centuries—military conflict and conquests, and the cruelty and economic oppression they underwent at the hands of more powerful neighbours. The prophecy looks towards a day when wrongs will be righted, the Lord's day when the nations will be gathered in the valley of Jehoshaphat to experience judgement (v. 2). Joel is very exercised by what were probably current or recent horrors—the scattering and enslavement of the people, the division of the land, trade in children and the looting of the nation's wealth (vv. 2–6)

Although the prophecy looks towards the judgement of 'all the nations' (v. 2), it addresses particular neighbours—the Phoenician trading cities, Tyre and Sidon, with Greece also mentioned as the destination of the slaves. The prophet Amos had already condemned the trade in human beings between Tyre and Edom (Amos 1:9), and Ezekiel had lamented Tyre's slave trade with the Greeks ('Javan': Ezekiel 27:13). It was, no doubt, a longstanding practice. However, the bitterness of Joel's prophecy, with its picture of the people of Judah having the satisfaction of buying Phoenician children and selling them on to the Sabeans, far away (v. 8), suggests immediate anger at current events.

In previous decades, Western Christians might have read this passage with a sense of disturbance about the vengeful message it holds, but now, when we are increasingly aware of modern slavery and the hideous trafficking of children stolen from war zones and the scenes of natural disasters, we may well share and sympathise with the emotions of revulsion and anger that lie behind it.

6 The valley of decision

Joel 3:8–21

Some evils do, indeed, cry to heaven. As Joel continues with the theme of the judgement of the nations, Edom and Egypt (v. 19) are added explicitly to the roll-call of those whose inhumanity to God's people will earn devastating punishment. However, this is in the context of prophecy foreseeing judgement on *all* the nations—and not just judgement but holy war against them in 'the valley of Jehoshaphat' (v. 12) or the 'valley of decision' (v. 14). 'Jehoshaphat' means 'The Lord has judged'; we do not know exactly where this valley was, but it was presumably in the neighbourhood of Jerusalem. The picture of the Lord roaring from Zion (v. 16), his voice overpowering the muttering tumult of the gathered multitudes, concurs with many other Old Testament prophecies about the Lord fighting for his people from the holy city. The idea that it is the Lord who has intentionally goaded the nations to gather against him there, driving them to turn their farming tools into weaponry, is a striking reversal of Isaiah's prophecy of Jerusalem as the peaceful city to which the nations will flow to learn from the Lord (Isaiah 2:2–4; echoed in Micah 4:1–4).

It is probably harder now to discuss 'holy war' prophecies in the Bible dispassionately than it was a few years ago, because we are increasingly aware that some members of another monotheistic religion espouse the 'holy war' tradition of their faith in an alarmingly literalistic way, with devastating consequences in the Middle East and elsewhere. For members of so-called Islamic State, there is a strong belief in a final battle against God's enemies at Dabiq, as prophesied in the Quran, and they seek to goad the nations into this apocalyptic encounter. If this way of reading texts by some members of another religion horrifies us, it should make us cautious in the handling of similar texts in our own scriptures. At least such passages may drive us to prayer, if only to confess before God our own difficulties in interpreting them.

As Christians we can remember Jesus' picture of the Son of Man coming to sit in judgement when 'all the nations will be gathered before him' (Matthew 25:32). This illustrates the criteria on which the Lord's judgement—whatever form it takes—will be based.

Guidelines

The prophecy of the book of Joel deals with perennial issues, but in ways in which we, as Christians today, might not naturally approach them.

- Natural and environmental disaster: Joel calls the people not to be in denial about the disaster overtaking them, but to solve the problem by responding with prayer and penitence. We too, in the face of issues such as climate change, agricultural failures and epidemics, need not to be in denial. However, our society believes that the proper response is to change human practices that ravage the earth, while researching ways to take a measure of control over some of nature's destructive forces, such as locusts, disease-bearing mosquitoes or flooding. Where might prayer come into our response to disaster?

- Corporate prayer: A secularised society such as ours seems an unlikely context for calls to national prayer, and yet the spiritual need to join together with a common focus on human suffering continues to manifest itself in practices such as a minute's commemorative silence. Christian organisations continue, also, to call their followers to shared times of prayer and intercession for different purposes, and sometimes for the whole nation. What is your experience of such shared spiritual acts, and what do you think their value is?

- Democracy of the Spirit: Joel prophesied the manifestation of spiritual gifts by 'all flesh' (2:28), and Peter claimed that this was fulfilled in the early church at Pentecost. In your experience, what enables such a 'democracy of the Spirit', what holds it back, and what blessings (or dangers) does it promise?

• Vengeance: The human instinct to hope for revenge is very strong, and is given voice in Joel's prophecy of the disasters to be visited on those who mistreated Israel. What place does the idea of 'just deserts' have in a Christian view of justice, and in Christian hope and prayer?

• Holy war: In what sense can a Christian believe in 'holy war', and how can we teach with integrity from biblical passages that describe or foresee it?

FURTHER READING

William A. Anderson, *Hosea, Joel, Amos, Obadiah, Jonah, Micah, Nahum, Habakkuk, Zephanaiah, Haggai, Zechariah, Malachi* (Liguori Catholic Bible Study), Liguori, 2014.

John J. Collins, *Joel, Obadiah, Haggai, Zechariah, Malachi* (New Collegeville Bible Commentary), Liturgical Press, 2012.*

Joyce G. Baldwin, *Haggai, Zechariah, Malachi* (Tyndale Bible Commentary), IVP, 1972.*

Paula Gooder, *Hosea to Micah* (The People's Bible Commentary), BRF, 2005.*

David L. Petersen, *Haggai and Zechariah 1—8* (Old Testament Library), SCM, 1984.

Paul L. Redditt, *Haggai, Zechariah, Malachi* (New Century Bible Commentary), Eerdmans, 1995.

Pieter A. Verhoeff, *The Books of Haggai and Malachi* (New International Bible Commentary), Eerdmans, 1987.

* More popular commentaries

Mission and the Holy Spirit

In the September–December 2016 issue of *Guidelines* I began to look at how the mission of the church is shaped by the life of Christ. Initially, we explored mission in the light of the incarnation. In January–April 2017 we took two weeks to look at mission in the light of the cross and resurrection. Now, in this final week of studies, we look at mission in the company of the Holy Spirit.

The Holy Spirit is, as many would acknowledge, the least accessible member of the Trinity, less familiar to us than the Father or Jesus himself. This is hardly surprising, as the images of Father and Son connect more readily with us than does the imagery of breath, dove, wind or flame. We need to go deeper, therefore, past the imagery, to try to connect with the mysterious reality that is the Spirit of God.

Bishop John V. Taylor, in his wonderful book *The Go-Between God*, reminds us that this imagery is necessary because it represents 'experience which only images can adequately convey'. This week, therefore, our studies will focus largely on the lived experience of Jesus first and foremost, and the experience of God's people living in communion with the Holy Spirit. By asking, 'What was the experience of Jesus and the early church?' we will reflect on our own experiences, real and anticipated, and thereby gain an experiential rather than theoretical understanding of the Holy Spirit.

This, I believe, is a worthy aim, but I am acutely aware that as we wrestle with and learn together about God the Holy Spirit, we must not make the mistake of placing mental acuity before prayerful submission. The privilege and duty to pray is paramount to understanding. This combination of study and prayer will necessarily lead us to encounter a trinitarian theology of mission—a rich and complex movement, originating in God and finding its fulfilment in God, a movement into which we are invited to participate, by faith through grace. Such is the mission we are invited to join, first as beneficiaries of God's saving grace, and then as ambassadors of the king of heaven—Father, Son and Holy Spirit.

Biblical quotations are taken from the New Revised Standard Version unless stated otherwise.

1 The Holy Spirit: God with us

John 14:11–31

At Christmas the word 'Immanuel' trips off the tongue—God with us. On other occasions we claim the promise given by Moses to Joshua that '[the Lord] will be with you; he will not fail you or forsake you' (Deuteronomy 31:8), reiterated in Joshua 1:5 with the words, 'I will not fail you or forsake you.'

The fact that it is actually the Holy Spirit who is with us is often overlooked. But Jesus makes this statement plainly, promising that the Spirit will come when he asks it of the Father, and that the Spirit will be with us for ever, abiding with us and living in us (John 14:16–17).

Here, then, is an explicitly trinitarian statement, showing how Father, Son and Spirit interplay to empower and protect those who look to them in faith. And yet, even in that very moment, we see that the three move and act in absolute union, for Jesus says, 'I am in the Father and the Father is in me' (v. 11) and, a few verses later, 'I am in my Father, and you in me, and I in you' (v. 20).

As this mesmerising movement oscillates from one to three, and three to one, and seems to open its embrace to include us (v. 21), it is the Holy Spirit who makes the divine dance possible. The Holy Spirit is the one who embodies Jesus with us, Jesus who is in the Father and in whom the Father is found. Only in this way can we hold together the unity of the Trinity.

In mission, knowing that 'God is with us' is of fundamental importance. Whether we are sharing our faith with a friend, puzzling over a community's brokenness, beyond our human ability to repair, or making decisions about whether to 'leave everything' to follow Jesus, knowing that God is here and engaged in the moment is vital.

At that moment, what matters is not our human giftedness, our problem-solving abilities or our innate optimism. It is the presence of God that matters. The God once found in human form in Jesus is still present in those who are children of faith, now by his Holy Spirit. Mission is suddenly not just possible, but thrilling. The one who breathed new life into us now takes our breath away.

2 The inner work of the Spirit

The excitement of knowing that God is with us may trigger a headlong dash to develop a missional mindset. But here we must pause for a moment, for we are first the objects of God's mission and only then participants in it. To be the object of God's mission is to accept the need for a lifelong process of discipleship and sanctification.

In an admittedly contested passage (it is unclear whether Paul is talking about his pre-conversion life or his present experience), the apostle confesses that he wrestles with sin himself (Romans 7:14–25). In writing to the church in Corinth, pointing out that they routinely wrong and defraud each other (1 Corinthians 6:7–8) and end up in court together, he appears to know the reality of the struggle that they, and we, live with.

The Corinthian believers have forgotten that they themselves are a place of habitation for the Holy Spirit (v. 19). Paul reminds them that they have been 'washed... sanctified... justified in the name of the Lord Jesus Christ and in the Spirit of our God' (v. 11) and adds for good measure, 'You were bought with a price; therefore glorify God in your body' (v. 20).

We can too easily lose sight of the need to become more Christ-like, both in behaviour (vv. 12–16) and in character (Galatians 5:22–23). These qualities are not peripheral to mission; they are part of our mission. By developing as disciples, we become better ambassadors for Christ.

Thankfully, Jesus anticipated this struggle and promised the sending of the Holy Spirit, whom he describes with the Greek word *parakletos* (John 16:7). Variously translated as helper, counsellor, comforter and advocate, each word expresses the idea of a companion.

But the Holy Spirit is more than an accompanier, remarkable though that idea is. There is a functional side to the presence of the Holy Spirit, for Jesus says that he 'will guide you into all the truth' (John 16:13). Here also there is a rich description, for 'the Spirit of truth... will take what is mine and declare it to you. All that the Father has is mine' (John 16:13–15).

Once again, in this divine work of sanctification, we find that the Spirit is the one who enables Father and Son also to be active in our lives.

3 The leading of the Holy Spirit

Acts 15:1–29

Theology and mission are inextricably intertwined. The theological convictions surrounding Jesus' death and resurrection catapulted the first believers into the mission of preaching and teaching, and so the kingdom of God expanded. That theology-driven mission took the church to a boundary place where God's kingdom and the kingdoms of the world met, which necessitated a reworking of aspects of its theology. While the core of the faith remained unchanged, God's Spirit was preparing to reveal new truths.

In Acts 15, the mission of the church has reached a boundary place. Gentiles are becoming believers and the church leaders are trying to work out whether the Jewish laws are to be made mandatory for them. God has prepared Peter for this moment through his encounter with Cornelius, climaxing in the gift of the Holy Spirit being poured out on Gentiles (Acts 10).

Now they gather in Jerusalem for a historic Council, and first Peter (v. 7), then Paul and Barnabas (v. 12) tell of the gift of the Holy Spirit being given to the Gentiles. James then takes the lead and, in verses 15–17, links the testimony of the brothers with the words of the Prophets, quoting Amos 9:11–12, apparently from the Septuagint. (See John Stott's *The Message of Acts* for an excellent explanation of the textual problem here.) A renewed theology emerges, a letter is formulated and messengers go out with the news that 'it has seemed good to the Holy Spirit and to us to impose on you no further burden...' (v. 28).

Here we see the evidence of theology sparking mission, and mission demanding a courageous reexamination of theology. All is done in good order, with wise leadership, scriptural reflection and, above all, the communal discernment of the Holy Spirit.

To this day, mission and theology enjoy the same interplay. In past generations, missionaries encountered polygamy in Africa and caste divisions in India, and had to formulate fresh theological responses to new situations. Today, when the church engages with politics, science, economics or the arts, we need to explore each in the light of both inherited and emerging theological insight, and not be afraid to do so. Sexuality, IVF, climate change, genetic screening and assisted dying are also issues where the church needs to debate wisely, study scripture deeply and discern the mind of Christ through the Holy Spirit.

40

29 May–4 June

4 The power of the Holy Spirit

Luke 4:1–21

The power of the Holy Spirit was evident at every step in the life of Jesus. The Holy Spirit brought life, literally, at the annunciation (Luke 1:35). When Jesus was baptised, the Holy Spirit descended upon him (Luke 3:22) and marked him out as the Son of God. At the beginning of his ministry he was led into the wilderness (Luke 4:1) and emerged full of Holy Spirit power (v. 14). When he preached, he knew the Spirit to be upon him and anointing him (v. 18).

We also see the impact of the power of the Holy Spirit in the life of the early apostles, including Stephen (Acts 7:55), Philip (8:29), Saul of Tarsus and Ananias (9:17–18) and Agabus (11:28).

It would be easy to overlook the fact that, for the early church, when someone came to faith it was observed as a powerful experience. Often it was the act of speaking in tongues that stood out (Acts 10:45–46) while Barnabas and Paul spoke of 'signs and wonders… among the Gentiles' (15:12).

Even when we are powerless, when we have nothing left to give or say, exhausted and spent, the Holy Spirit is there for us, interceding 'with sighs too deep for words' (Romans 8:26). Throughout history, right up to today, the transformative power of the Holy Spirit has equipped the saints for witness and service. But there is a challenge here, and it's a very obvious one. We come to faith with a set of experiences and a combination of knowledge, skills and character. These qualities will form and shape our identity and the way our faith is outworked, but our giftedness can dull the craving for the transforming power of the Holy Spirit that will truly set us apart.

Understandably, therefore, Paul's prayer for the young church in Ephesus was that the Father 'may grant that you may be strengthened in your inner being with power through his Spirit' (Ephesians 3:16). This needs to be our heartbreaking cry for ourselves: 'Lord, strengthen me in my inner being with power through your Holy Spirit.' May that prayer never cease.

5 Free and assured: the gift of the Holy Spirit

Ephesians 1:1–14

Our language is peppered with expressions that caution us not to expect too much from life, such as 'No such thing as a free lunch.' And even if we do receive such a gift, we don't expect it to last: 'Here today, gone tomorrow!' These ideas may not seem important to us, but, for millions in today's world, they matter. To the poor, the abused, the downtrodden and those who, for whatever reason, live with guilt or hopelessness, the possibility of something free and assured can be literally life-changing.

Ephesians 2:8 tells us that 'by grace you have been saved through faith, and this is not your own doing; it is the gift of God', and, as if that wasn't enough, 'When you believed, you were marked in him with a seal, the promised Holy Spirit, who is a deposit guaranteeing our inheritance' (1:13–14, NIV). The mission of the church encapsulates this free and enduring gift—and it is the agency of the Holy Spirit that makes it possible, from the breath of life that regenerates the dead (Ephesians 2:1, 4–5) to the power that holds us even in the face of death (Romans 8:38–39).

These great truths, that the gospel is a free gift that cannot be earned, and that the life it gives is irrevocable, shape our approach to mission. So we must never consider anyone beyond the reach of God, quietly nurturing the prejudice that he or she doesn't deserve the gift of faith. No one does. That's the point. It's a free gift!

But assurance is vital too. Those whose faith once burned brightly can find themselves struggling to believe. Pastorally, while we long for people to rediscover the joy of full assurance and should do all we can to encourage it, we shouldn't see present doubting necessarily as an indication that their once-strong faith was not real. Yet we will strive to bring them back home to the heart of the Father, that they may know his peace again.

Finally, this 'free and assured' good news draws us deeper into worship of God. The sinner's cry is met with the divine embrace, full forgiveness and adoption into the family of God. The resultant assurance reminds us that 'the chief end of man [sic] is to glorify God and enjoy him forever' (Westminster Shorter Catechism).

6 The missionary life

The second letter of Peter is an oft-neglected epistle and yet the first chapter offers us a wonderful call to lead a Spirit-enabled, mission-focused life, lived to the glory of God. In verse 3 we are told that the power of Jesus 'has given us everything needed for life and godliness'. What an extraordinary statement! Peter explains that 'everything' means 'his precious and very great promises' (v. 4), which help us to grow as disciples.

Growth like this 'will keep you from being ineffective and unfruitful' (v. 8). Peter reminds his readers that he was an eyewitness of Jesus (v. 16), so the prophetic word he shares with them is 'fully confirmed' (v. 19). He reaches the climax of the chapter by pointing away from himself: 'no prophecy of scripture is a matter of one's own interpretation'. Prophecy comes not from the human will but from 'men and women moved by the Holy Spirit [who] spoke from God' (vv. 20–21).

Here, then, is the visible, present-day connection between the Holy Spirit and our mission in Jesus' name. The good news of Jesus Christ, crucified and risen, is the heart of our mission, and it comes embodied in those who are redeemed and moved by the Holy Spirit, speaking as from the presence of God. This is how the scriptures themselves came about. This is how the same word of God comes alive in our mission endeavour, when it is spoken and enacted by those who come from God, 'moved by the Holy Spirit'.

It is as we cultivate our relationship with God, through prayer and scripture reading, through Christian fellowship and the personal discipline of holy living, that we find ourselves immersed in God's presence. From God's presence we emerge into school and workshop, neighbourhood and office, demonstrating in word and action the potential of God's transforming power in our communities.

Here we see the mysterious dance of the triune God again. God the Holy Spirit is with us, and we seek to nurture a disciplined life that leads us consciously into the presence of God. Then it is as if we emerge from the enriching presence of God to go into all the world. Yet, even as we go, God is with us always, never forsaking us.

God is mystery, of course, which is why our words get tangled. Images, at first glance less impressive, are actually more able to capture the nuances we long to convey.

Guidelines

- The Holy Spirit was with you as you opened your eyes this morning, as you breathe right now, and as you face the tasks to come. Reflect for a moment on what that feels like.
- We all know the struggle of daily life, our high aspirations set against our humble achievements, but we are reminded to 'glorify God in [our] body' (1 Corinthians 6:20). Reflect on that for a moment and pray.
- Consider an area where your theological views have changed over the years. Do you sense that God is leading you to reexamine other areas in the light of your mission?
- The power of the Holy Spirit was much discussed in the heyday of the charismatic movement, but maybe less so today. That's not helpful. Consider for a moment where you need the power of God's Spirit in your life or ministry.
- Are you assured in your faith, safe and secure, held by the God from whom no one can separate you? If so, what implication does that have for your missional mindset? If you are in doubt, revisit Ephesians 1 and 2, read and pray, and ask the Holy Spirit to fill you again.
- Pray: 'Holy Spirit—breath of life, dove of peace, gentle breeze and dancing flame—come close and abide. Impart your power, that in my weakness I may yet serve the Lord who saved me and sends me, to the glory of my Father in heaven. Amen

FURTHER READING

John Stott, *The Message of Acts* (The Bible Speaks Today), IVP, 1990.

J.V. Taylor, *The Go-Between God: The Holy Spirit and the Christian mission*, SCM Classics, 2002.

K. Ward, *Christ and the Cosmos: A reformulation of trinitarian doctrine*, Cambridge University Press, 2015.

Matthew 19—23

The chapters we are about to study offer us a wide range of insights into the character, teaching and career of Jesus the Messiah. A one-dimensional view of Jesus is not possible once we have encountered him in a diversity of settings and encounters. We shall see him as a compassionate figure who is readily moved in the face of human suffering and pleading, healing the blind and gathering in the excluded. We shall observe him speaking and acting with tenderness towards the little children, laying his hands on them and blessing them. We will find him grieving and weeping over the city of Jerusalem for its recalcitrance. We shall learn from him as a brilliant if, at times, enigmatic storyteller and as a faithful interpreter of the Hebrew scriptures. We shall notice the fierce and intimidating ways in which he debated with the religious groupings of his day, giving as good as he got. We shall see him physically overturning tables in the temple.

Perhaps we shall be surprised at the number of parables in which Jesus refers to shocking outcomes, such as being put to a miserable death (21:41), the destruction and burning of a city (22:7), being cast into outer darkness (22:13). It will certainly surprise us that Jesus once more makes reference to 'hell' (23:15; see also 5:22, 29–30; 10:28; 23:33). This is a word that might be translated more exactly as 'Gehenna'. It is based on the place adjacent to Jerusalem that was used as the city's rubbish tip, a place of continual burning and of putrefaction (Isaiah 66:24). It became a symbol of God's judgement in 'the world to come'. We cannot delight in this dimension of Jesus' preaching, since eternal judgement is something to regret, not celebrate. But neither should we ignore it if we wish to have a rounded and accurate knowledge of Jesus and his way.

Jesus certainly made use of various rhetorical devices in order to communicate effectively. It is good advice not to take everything he said literally (see 5:29–30 as an example). But everything that comes to us from him, whether in word or deed, does need to be taken extremely seriously if we are to be true to him.

Quotations are taken from the New Revised Standard Version.

1 Stable, faithful, permanent

Matthew 19:1–12

Jesus is now in the part of Judah on the eastern side of the Jordan, apparently avoiding Samaria. Once more he is in contention with scribes and Pharisees, who press him as to where he stands on divorce. In the Judaism of the day, there were two schools of thought, one more strict than the other. Jesus identifies with the stricter school: divorce should happen, if at all, only in the most extreme circumstances (v. 9) and not for trivial reasons. Mosaic law permitted divorce only because humans are hard-hearted and create big problems for themselves. Sometimes, there were no viable alternatives. Divorced Hebrew wives were entitled to a proper 'certificate of divorce' (Deuteronomy 24:1–4). Presumably this was to allow them to marry again, which mere survival would probably dictate.

It is of interest to note how Jesus reasoned from scripture in this case. He cites two foundational texts and combines them to shape his argument (Genesis 1:27; 2:24). In other words, he goes back to what is known of the divine purpose for men and women in creation, that they should be joined together physically and spiritually to become as one. The biblical vision therefore is not for divorce but for marriages that remain stable, faithful and permanent and so become fruitful not only in the bearing of children but in the fostering of a lifetime of love. The vision is not always fulfilled, because of natural tragedies like premature death or the human capacity to generate breakdowns. But the divine intent should not for this reason be taken lightly; it should be kept as a realisable ideal.

This is not to say that marriage is compulsory. Although the continuance of the human race depends on the passing on of our genes, a celibate single life is an equally honourable estate. Jesus more than adequately demonstrated this, as did the apostle Paul after him (we think). This is the intent of the discussion about eunuchs in verses 10–12. Those who have 'made themselves eunuchs' is not to be taken literally—it is an example of Jesus' use of hyperbole—but is a way of speaking of a consecrated celibate life 'for the sake of the kingdom of heaven' (v. 12). This too, like marriage, can be a gift of God and, in Jesus' day, was unusual.

2 Jesus and the children

Like some other adults, the disciples clearly saw the children as a bit of a nuisance, from whom Jesus needed to be protected. By contrast, Jesus was delightfully open to them and their parents, and so these short verses offer us a wonderful scene. Being celibate by no means signifies dislike of children. Quite the reverse: there is love to spare. Here Jesus is keen that they should come to him and that, through the laying on of his hands, they should receive his blessing and prayer (v. 13). The kingdom of God belongs to them and those who, in their receptivity, are like them (see also 18:1–5). Of course children should be brought to Jesus and are always free to come to him. In that, Jesus is himself the revelation of the Father (11:27). We can therefore say that this is how the Father perceives, loves and welcomes children. This is no insignificant statement, given the high rates of child mortality in the history of the human race. In the light of these verses, those who grieve the loss of their young children need have no anxiety about where they stand with God through his Son.

If they are to be true to their Lord, the churches that confess him ought to be as child-friendly as he was—safe communities where the youngest receive both blessing and prayer. For some communities, this is expressed in the service of infant baptism (although, to be precise, it does not say here that Jesus baptised the children). For others, it is shown in services of infant presentation and blessing. Although these practices are not specifically instituted in the New Testament, the verses here provide the blessing of the children with adequate justification. These ceremonies point to the broader reality of providing a loving space into which the young may be brought.

There is also a personal challenge about our attitudes to the young. A wise African saying is that it takes a whole village to raise a child. The responsibility of parenting is a heavy one to carry in isolation. Children need Christ-like figures beyond their immediate families who will prepare them for the challenges of life. If Jesus sets a wonderful example for us, the stern speaking and attitude of the disciples (v. 13) is definitely something to avoid.

3 The eye of the needle

This is a rich passage that invites many questions. The rich and privileged young man who approaches Jesus is anxious about what to do to obtain eternal life (v. 16), or 'the life of the world to come', as other Jews would have put it. Jesus sets out not to make it easy for him. He plays him along. Perhaps the point about keeping the commandments to enter into life (v. 17) is his way of exposing the fact that eternal life comes through faith and not by works (Ephesians 2:8). At any rate, in his interrogation Jesus leaves out the command not to covet and, in so doing, pinpoints where the young man was falling short of perfection (v. 21). The man had a problem with love of possessions, and this was blocking the way to life.

The rich never got off lightly when they encountered Jesus. They are likely, he said, to find it the hardest to enter into the kingdom of heaven. In fact, Jesus contrasts the largest beast that would have been known to his hearers with the smallest aperture of which they would have been aware, and says that getting the one through the other is as likely to happen as a rich person entering the kingdom. That does not leave much hope for many of us, then or now, as the disciples rightly understood (v. 25). Our only hope is that what is impossible for us actually becomes possible when we factor in God (v. 26). This is the good news of salvation. What we are incapable of doing, God is able to make happen.

It is not the tally of our works that will save us: all of us, like the rich young man, are deficient at some point, even at all points. What counts is trusting in and following after the one who has come from God to reverse our fortunes. He is our hope for abundant life in the age to come (v. 28). Forsaking our attachment to and trust in riches and possessions for the sake of Christ is a very small price to pay for what awaits us in his company, both in the present life and in the next. This is God's strange way of doing things (v. 30), and it is because God is good (v. 17).

4 Divine generosity

The fact that Matthew 19:30, which immediately precedes this parable, and 20:16, which ends it, correspond so closely in thought perhaps indicates what the parable means. With Jesus, the usual order of things is turned upside down. In the parable, the owner of the vineyard does nothing wrong. He agrees a daily price with his labourers (v. 2) and that is what they receive at the end of the day, as standard practice dictated (v. 10). Yet they have some cause to grumble, since two further groups of workers who arrive late on the scene are each paid exactly the same. Most workers would feel aggrieved by this. But still, the owner has done nothing wrong. He has acted both righteously and generously and, as he says in a key verse, is fully at liberty to do what he wants with what is his own (v. 15). This is an irrefutable argument. Perhaps he sees that the workers who came late were near destitution and has acted compassionately.

Behind the parable is Jesus' own explanation of his ministry to the poor and the despised. He shows kindness towards those who have not 'worked' for it. He heals and liberates, regardless of whether people 'deserve' it. He treats his disciples with equal respect, whether they have borne 'the burden of the day and the scorching heat' (v. 12) or whether they have joined him but lately. Beyond Jesus, too, there is another reality that his ministry reflects: it is the generosity of God. God does not treat us according to what we deserve but according to the 'immeasurable riches of his grace' (Ephesians 2:7), with which the divine nature is full. God can do what God wishes with that which is God's own. God will always do what is right but, beyond that, will do what is generous—more than fair—even to the point of breaking whatever rules we invent.

The parable begins with Jesus saying, 'For the kingdom of heaven is like…'. It gives us an important insight into the divine nature, upon which the whole New Testament builds. We call it grace, and it is embodied in Jesus.

5 Greatness and service

Matthew 20:17–28

The passage begins with Jesus' third prediction of his passion, following on from Matthew 16:21–23 and 17:22–23. This time there are added details: Jesus will be handed over to the Gentiles (Romans) to be mocked, flogged and crucified (v. 19). As the day draws nearer, so the details become clearer to Jesus. There is great courage here. There are also the beginnings of a theology of atonement in verse 28. The Son of Man has come as a servant and will give his life as 'a ransom for many'. A ransom is a price paid in order to set someone free, perhaps a prisoner of war or an enslaved person. Christ's death is the price to be paid to set Israel free, but from what? From captivity to death, sin, evil or oppression? The details are yet to be made known but the significance of Jesus' death as a saving event is indicated.

Once more the disciples are shown in a poor light. While Jesus wrestles with momentous realities, James and John the sons of Zebedee (4:21) and their mother are pondering their own prospects in the coming kingdom. If the other ten are angry about this (v. 24), it is surely because they too are jostling for position. Once more, Jesus reverses the order of things. Concern for worldly prominence and power is something the pagan Gentiles have, but it is emphatically not his way, nor should it be theirs (v. 26). 'Lording it' over others and acting like tyrants is a constant human problem, pointing to the self-exaltation that lies at the heart of sin. Not even the church has been able to escape this snare. The humility of the way of Christ is apparently foreign to us.

As to the question of whether they can 'drink the cup' and their foolish answer (v. 22), they reveal how little understanding they have even now. Yes, they will be able to drink the cup, in that they too will share Jesus' suffering (v. 23), but they can never share in the reality of the cross as a liberating sacrifice. This is for Christ alone. In the event, those on the right and left of Jesus turn out to be two crucified thieves (27:38), an ironic commentary on the nature of the Son of Man's kingdom and of his 'throne'.

6 Asking rightly

Matthew 20:29–34

Mark 10:46–52 tells of blind Bartimaeus being healed at Jericho, and this account in Matthew bears many similarities to that event, except that here there are two blind beggars, not one. It is possible that, despite the similarities, this is a different occasion (it would not be unusual for two or more beggars to sit together). Alternatively, for economy of space, Matthew may have doubled up in this account to incorporate a different such healing. The way the blind men cry for mercy to the 'Lord, Son of David' with such urgency is both striking and moving. So is the way Jesus is moved with compassion and heals them with his touch (v. 34).

In today's world we have learnt ways of coping with blindness and have developed disciplines in which the visually impaired can live full, productive and satisfying lives. Such equality would have been hard to achieve in Jesus' day and the disabled of all kinds would have been pushed to the margins, often reliant upon the charity of others. To be blind was to be excluded from the life and worship of the community. Jesus' acts of healing, therefore, were more than just acts of compassion overcoming disease or disability. They involved restoration to community life and worship, inclusion within the commonwealth of Israel. When we think of healing today, we often miss these aspects of well-being and think only of relief from personal suffering. Jesus was doing a greater thing than we imagine for the people.

There is something to be learned from the question that Jesus posed to the two men: 'What do you want me to do for you?' (see also John 5:6). We might imagine that the answer was obvious. But it is good to ask, and when we ask, it is good to be specific. To identify and name our needs before God helps us to receive an answer. There is no doubt here that the men were dealing with real needs and not just superficial 'wants'. When the answer came, it was clear from whom it had come and what form it took. 'You do not have, because you do not ask', wrote James. 'You ask and do not receive, because you ask wrongly, in order to spend what you get on your pleasures' (James 4:2–3).

Guidelines

This week's readings have offered a series of glimpses into Jesus' earthly ministry, and at all points we have been presented with a uniquely thoughtful and compassionate figure. It was once held by some scholars that because they were largely composed of narratives and stories, the Gospels were to be contrasted unfavourably with the epistles, which were felt to be superior because they contained argument and, above all, doctrine. If anything, the pendulum has now swung the other way, with great esteem being given to the power of narrative to inform, shape and intrigue. We ought also to say that the Gospels come to us in the form of embodied or narrated doctrine. We have seen how the love of God for the young shines through the welcome and blessing that Jesus gave to the children. We have noted the divine compassion expressed through Jesus in the case of the two blind men. We have seen in Jesus' prediction of his passion the outlines of a doctrine of atonement. We have been faced with the doctrine of God's grace in the parable of the workers in the vineyard. We have learnt that it is impossible for humans to enter into eternal life by virtue of their works, but that what is impossible for us is possible with God. If Jesus is the way, the truth and the life (John 14:6), it is because he is the very incarnation of all these realities.

Older generations of theological thinkers were apt to refer to their writings as a 'body of divinity', but the only true body of divinity is the one we have been reading about in these chapters. Jesus Christ is the life of God lived out in human form, humbly and graciously in the midst of human existence. In effect, the New Testament epistles, with all their theological reflections and doctrinal explanations, are nothing more or less than inspired attempts to spell out the meaning of what was present for us in Jesus. They search for the best language and thought forms available to them to express the inexpressible, to expound the 'immeasurable riches of [God's] grace in kindness towards us in Christ Jesus' (Ephesians 2:7). Thanks be to God.

1 A good day's work

Matthew 21:1–17

As the Gospel moves toward its climax, Jesus continues to act in provocative ways. This incident (which is remembered by Christians on 'Palm' Sunday even though palms are not mentioned here, only cloaks and branches) is in the nature of an acted parable. The evidence suggests that Jesus has prearranged this moment and knows exactly what he is doing. The donkey is password-protected (vv. 2–3). By dramatising his entry into Jerusalem, he is making a claim to a certain kind of kingship. The Old Testament background that supports his claim is mentioned in verse 5 (see Zechariah 9:9), and the shouts of acclamation in verse 9 are drawn from Psalm 118:25–26. The kind of kingship Jesus embodies is that of a humble servant who rides not on a war-horse but on a donkey. Here we see him continuing to reinterpret the nature of messiah-kingship. The crowds receive him both as the Son of David and as 'the prophet Jesus from Nazareth in Galilee' (vv. 9, 11). It is good to receive him under these titles and more.

What Jesus does in the temple is quite shocking. In effect, he paralyses the whole temple system for a time, and with the use of brute force, making the offering of sacrifices impossible. This was his protest. It is possible to infer that he was objecting to financial exploitation of the people in the changing of currency for the Tyrian silver shekels that were required in the temple, and to the temple management that may have been taking a rake-off (vv. 12–13). A den of robbers is, after all, a place where thieves gather and feel safe (Jeremiah 7:11). Here would be a condemnation of the religious scams that have, sadly, been found throughout history, even in Christianity. In view of his reference to the temple as a house of prayer, however, it is more likely that he is protesting against the use of the extensive Court of the Gentiles for buying and selling (v. 12) instead of providing a place where all the Gentiles could come to pray (Isaiah 56:6–7). Jesus was restoring the temple to its proper use as a place of open access for the healing of the blind and lame and the sincere praise of God (vv. 14–16).

2 Another acted parable

Matthew 21:18–27

Some find the cursing of the fig tree problematic because it might cast Jesus in a rather petulant light. In fact, it is a further deliberate acted parable and speaks of the failure of the nation of Israel to bear the fruit it should. Jesus was hungry for a responsive and righteous people and not for food alone (v. 18). He was destined to be disappointed on both counts.

Mark 11:12–25 divides this incident into two parts, with the cleansing of the temple in between, and so makes the reference clear. The fig tree is Israel, and it has a display of leaves but is barren of fruit. Religion can sometimes be utterly void of virtue. Judgement therefore falls on Israel's religious system. Faith in Jesus is what counts.

The reference to prayer and the removal of mountains (Matthew 21:21) might be seen not simply as generalised commentary on the power of faith, but as an ironic reference to the Temple Mount, which would have been plainly visible from the Mount of Olives (21:1). Near the place where Jesus was standing at this point, the Roman legions would encamp when they came to destroy both temple and city in AD70. Jesus considered that the rejection of the non-violent way he advocated would lead to these disastrous events, as in due time we shall see (23:37–39). His words are evidence of his confidence that he was doing the will of God even though he was opposed by the religious system.

That clash of cultures then appears as Jesus argues with the official leaders of the Jewish establishment. They want to know where his authority comes from (v. 23). In their eyes, Jesus had no authority because he was not a trained or accredited rabbi. He had not been through the system. The idea that he might have been raised up directly by God, outside the usual channels, had not occurred to them, or, if it had, it was unwelcome. But then the same was true of John the Baptist, as Jesus quickly identifies. By this time John had become something of a popular martyr and hero whose spiritual authority they were reluctant to contradict (v. 27).

3 What we say and what we do

Matthew 21:28–32

Having got the religious leaders in his sights, Jesus is relentless in pursuing his critique. Of the two sons (and they are sons), one says the wrong thing but does the right thing and the other says the right thing but does the wrong thing. The second son is thus branded both a liar and a hypocrite whose words are not matched by his deeds. What we say or think about ourselves is not necessarily what is true. So it was with the religious leaders, even though they belonged to God's inheritance, the people of Israel, and so had the privilege of sonship.

Jesus reflects here his own experience as one who has come from God. Those who might be expected to welcome him have failed to do so, but those who might be expected to refuse him, the 'tax collectors and prostitutes' (v. 31) who are beyond the pale of respectable religious devotion, are those who welcome him gladly. They are the ones most ready to respond to his message of the kingdom and so to enter it. What Jesus found to be true for himself, he also reckoned to be true of his predecessor, John the Baptist, thus exposing the fact that the hypocrisy of the unresponsive leaders was habitual. A habitual response becomes a prison in which people are confined (v. 32).

These words must be heard as a challenge to all who believe and belong to established patterns of faith, the kind of people who either write Bible study notes or read them. Our natural inclination is to reckon ourselves on the side of the tax collectors and prostitutes, the responsive and obedient people who, by dint of the fact, not least, that we read and study the Bible, are in 'the way of righteousness' (v. 32). Yet we are the ones more likely to be the hypocrites, since we know how to say the right thing but do not always live out what we say. Self-critical examination, leading to a change of mind, is what is required. The critical issue in the parable is doing the will of the Father (v. 31). What the Father wills is amply made known in the Son, who both does and says the right thing and whose willing example guides us into the way of truth.

4 The rejection of the son

Matthew 21:33–46
With this parable Jesus continues his scathing critique of the established leadership in Judah and its temple. The 'chief priests and the Pharisees' cannot evade the fact that he is directing his words at them (v. 45), although, to be fair, these two groups do need to be distinguished. The chief priests, of the Sadducee party, represented the establishment in ways that the Pharisees did not.

It is often said that a parable has one main point to make, but this one is more in the nature of an allegory. The vineyard is Israel, which has been usurped by those who think they have ownership of the nation. The slaves or servants who are sent to collect the true owner's produce are the prophets, who were continually rejected and ill-treated (v. 35). The son is Jesus himself, who will shortly be rejected and killed outside the city walls (v. 39). The rather bloodthirsty fate that results from the usurpers' actions is a prediction of the destruction of the temple. Rejecting Jesus is a fatal thing to do (v. 44) and will lead to a transfer of the divine purpose from Israel as a whole to the community, including many Israelites, that does welcome him as the holy one of God (v. 43).

In the course of this incident, Jesus draws upon a highly significant passage: Psalm 118:22–23. Jesus is like a stone that the builders reject because it does not seem to fit. The words and actions of Jesus that we have seen have alienated him from the movers and shakers in Israel (despite, or perhaps because of, his popularity with the ordinary people). Yet the rejected one is destined to undergo a dramatic and amazing reversal of fortunes to become either the capstone or the cornerstone of the building. The word can be translated both ways, and implies either that Jesus will be the foundation of a new temple or that he will be the stone that completes the temple God is already building. Perhaps both meanings are intended, and, either way, the crucial significance of Jesus is in view. The same words are used to interpret the resurrection in both Acts 4:11 and 1 Peter 2:7. The rejected one will become the exalted one. With God all things are possible, especially when they concern his Son.

5 Come on in!

Matthew 22:1–14

The parable of the wedding banquet appears to have two parts and two different lessons, one about inclusion and the other about exclusion. Imagining God's kingdom as a wedding feast has roots in the great final banquet portrayed in Isaiah 25:6–8 and repeated in Revelation 19:7–10. For Jesus, the great feast is already taking place (v. 2) and there is an open invitation to join it. To refuse such an invitation is a gross insult to its host, and yet that is the surprising and irrational response received by the king. The banquet is open to all and promises to be full of good things to be enjoyed (v. 4). Why should anybody ignore such lavish generosity and enjoyment? Yet the invitation is met with either apathy or hostility (vv. 5–6).

It takes us aback that Jesus, who espoused non-violence, used such violent images in his parables as those used in verse 7 to express the king's rage. The dramatic effect on his hearers must have been profound and his meaning hard to miss. If Israel's religious leaders were so dismissive of God's invitation into the kingdom, then the doors would be opened to all and sundry, even those who would never be considered candidates, and certainly including the Gentile nations. The king would make sure the wedding banquet was not wasted.

Jesus preached and lived a message of radical inclusion, reflecting the all-embracing love of God. He held out little hope for the very religious people who imagined themselves to be favoured by God. It therefore comes as a bit of a jolt when the parable turns in a different direction (vv. 11–14). If all and sundry have been invited in unexpectedly, how is it that they are now expected to wear the proper clothes? If the parable is about an undeserved invitation to the undeserving, how can anyone be excluded? It is possible that these verses actually belong to a different parable and have been edited into this one—or perhaps the abrupt turn is deliberate so that nobody gets the wrong idea. Clothing can symbolise righteousness. To be in the kingdom, without any righteousness of our own, we need to be clothed with the righteousness that God gives (see Romans 13:12–14). This too is divine generosity.

6 Debates and conflicts

The traffic between Jesus and his Jewish debating partners was two-way. He could denounce them and they could return the 'compliment'. These passages are like a tag-wrestling contest in which Jesus is on his own, facing three groups who try to 'entrap him' in what he says: Pharisees, Herodians and Sadducees (vv. 15–16, 23). Normally these groups would be at logger-heads with each other, but against Jesus they make common cause.

The first debate is about paying the annual census tax of one denarius to Caesar. Nobody likes paying taxes, but, as Caesar's image was on the coinage, there are overtones here of idolatry and spiritual compromise. By asking his opponents to produce the coin, Jesus successfully subverts any accusation that, in paying the tax himself, he is compromising. He seems intensely relaxed about the whole affair, to the point of regarding payment as a non-issue. The rule of Caesar cannot be avoided but, like all govern-ments, is a temporary arrangement, to be abolished when God's kingdom finally arrives—so play along.

Much has been built on verse 21 but, in truth, the saying is enigmatic. We should give to Caesar what may be required but should give everything to God, and even Caesar belongs to God. Civil government has its necessary place, but not one that can replace God.

The second debate is about the practice of levirate marriage (Deutero-nomy 25:5–10), designed in the Hebrew scriptures both to protect widows and to preserve a family's land ownership. In seeking to refute the idea of bodily resurrection (which they could not find in the books of Moses), the Sadducee party reduce the practice to the level of the absurd. After her seven hypothetical husbands, we can feel some sympathy for the woman (v. 27). Jesus sees through the device and cuts to the quick: they are misusing scripture for their misguided ends and failing to reckon with the power of God (v. 29). The rules of this present life do not necessarily apply to the world that is to come, just as the life of angels does not conform to mundane realities (v. 30).

Jesus did not receive formal training as a rabbi, but it is evident from these encounters that he was a skilled debater and well versed both in knowledge of the scriptures and in God's power to do more than we can imagine.

Guidelines

How much does a person need to know in order to become a Christian? One response might be that all they need is faith, since 'by grace you have been saved through faith' (Ephesians 2:8). Faith was clearly important to Jesus, but even faith requires knowledge. We should know whom we trust and why we trust them. It is true that knowledge is not enough, but zeal without enlightenment is likely to be misplaced (Proverbs 19:2; Romans 10:2). The followers of Jesus should strive to know what they are speaking of, just as Jesus did himself.

Preaching is a staple part of church life and its object is to inspire and motivate believers. As a way of imparting knowledge, preaching has its limitations. It is common to distinguish between preaching and teaching. Although the boundary between them must be porous, the focus may differ. Teaching aims to instruct and inform, to lay solid foundations of understanding. It is as necessary as preaching. But there is a saying: 'Nobody has taught anything until somebody has learnt something.' Learning depends upon the will to learn, to absorb knowledge so that it is thoroughly processed through our own minds and becomes formative of who we are and what we do. It is clear from the texts we have studied that Jesus had fully learnt the ways of God, to the point where he could challenge other understandings and put forward his own insights with confidence and authority as the word of God. Although study of scripture is not the only way in which we learn, it is certainly one way and should form a primary part of our spiritual diet.

To be a disciple is to be a learner, to be eager to learn the ways of Christ and to acquire knowledge that can be transformed into personal communion with the one to whom we are committed. Knowledge, so understood, is a gateway to spiritual depth and maturity. As in all spheres of life, we should take responsibility for our own learning. It is a form of direct, personal engagement with the object of our spiritual hunger and desires, and it requires effort. Engaging our brains can even feel painful at times, but it bears fruit.

1 The greatest commandment

Matthew 22:34–40

The wrestling match continues, with the Pharisees now returning to the fray. The lawyer (v. 35) is an expert in the law of Moses, a theologian. Once more, the question is designed to test Jesus. Of the 613 commandments contained in the Hebrew scriptures, which was the most important? On Mount Sinai, Moses was given two tablets of stone (Exodus 32:15–16), inscribed with our duties to God and to each other. To the lawyer Jesus offers not two tablets but two commandments that epitomise those duties (v. 40).

What Jesus says here is not new. Both commandments are taken from the scriptures (Deuteronomy 6:4–5; Leviticus 19:18). The first is the Shema (from 'Hear, O Israel'), the basic affirmation that devout Jews would say, morning and evening. The lawyer would know the words perfectly well and there would be little to argue with in identifying love for God as the most important commandment for Jewish believers (as it is for Christians). Jesus passes the test. There is no higher duty or joy than to love God. Jesus was probably not the only teacher to combine these two commandments, yet familiarity is apt to blunt the challenge they contain. Love for God is to be whole-hearted, and, given the perennially divided state of the human heart by which we both love God and fail to do so, the words are a continuing stimulus to improve on our current position. Love for the God of Israel is our project. The word 'love' here translates *agape*, the Greek word that implies more than affection and points to an act of will and self-giving.

Familiar though the words of verse 37 may be, there is an interesting twist: Jesus changes them. For the word 'strength' in Deuteronomy 6:5 he substitutes the word 'mind' (all four terms, 'heart, soul, strength and mind', are combined in Mark 12:30). The variation would surely have been noticed immediately. Loving God with the mind suggests reflection upon who God is, what God has done, and how God can be glorified. The mind is the gateway to the heart, since, as we think about God, we are likely to be moved to love God more completely. Jesus is drawing us to simplicity and integration in our love for God. It is the simplest things that are usually the most profound.

2 David's Lord

Now it is Jesus' turn to interrogate the Pharisees. He uses a debating device that would have been common among the rabbis in their wrestling with scripture. Jesus was long used to these kinds of discussions (Luke 2:46–47). The ways of arguing are not so familiar to us—they may seem a bit contorted and so require some explanation—but in his own context they were very effective.

Jesus begins with some common ground: it is agreed that the Messiah is the son of David (v. 42; see 1:1). It is also a shared belief both that David was the author of Psalm 110 and that, in composing scripture, he did so by the inspiration of the Spirit (v. 43). So far, so good. If the Messiah, then, is David's son, how could David also call him 'my Lord', as in Psalm 110:1? How could he both pre-exist David and be his descendant? There is a dissonance here. The Pharisees have no answer, and, for a time, the testing of Jesus comes to an end (v. 46).

From this encounter we may deduce certain things about the way Jesus thought. Firstly, he clearly regarded the Hebrew Psalms as, in some sense, inspired by God; by inference, he no doubt believed the same about all the Hebrew scriptures. Secondly, he saw himself being spoken of in those same scriptures and interpreted himself and his mission in the light of what he found there. Without his coming out and saying so, there is evidence here that he both saw himself as David's son, the Messiah, and as the one whom the Lord addresses as 'lord' in the Psalm, who will in time sit at the right hand of God and reign until his enemies are defeated. Thirdly, although the crowds regarded him as a prophet (21:46), Jesus understood himself as a prophet and more. This is either overweening self-confidence or it happens to be true. There is a decision to be made.

The Pharisees could not resolve the dissonance involved in the Messiah's being simultaneously a descendant of David and David's superior as the pre-existent Lord. In his own person, Jesus had resolved the tension, and so can we. He is Israel's Messiah. He came from the Father's right hand and will one day be the universal ruler over everything that opposes his kingdom of truth and light.

3 What religious people should avoid

Matthew 23:1–12

Jesus continues his scathing criticism of the Pharisees. We almost feel sorry for them. He acknowledges that they know and teach the Torah (v. 2), but that is where all commendation ends. They do not live up to their teaching. They turn the Torah from the joy and delight it is meant to be (Psalm 119:97–104) into a series of harsh burdens.

Perhaps Jesus has in mind here the way the Pharisees extended and added to the biblical laws (v. 4). They liked (from his perspective) to parade their devotion before others by accentuating those things that marked them out as religious: the phylacteries (leather boxes containing words of scripture and worn on the forehead and arms during prayer) and prayer fringes on their garments (Deuteronomy 6:8–9). They loved open displays of deference (vv. 6–7) and titles of respect such as 'rabbi' (literally 'my great one'), 'father' and 'teacher'. All of these Jesus understood as subtle ways of exalting oneself rather than adopting the ethos of humility and self-effacement. They are displeasing to God (v. 12).

Behind these characteristics Jesus is identifying spiritual or religious pride, which is a besetting sin of the devout, especially the professional devout. When we have dealt with the more obvious and earthy sins in our lives, we become prey to more subtle forms. It is a bad thing to behave like animals but worse to behave like devils. The spiritual sins are more deadly than the bodily ones, but are less readily located. Spiritual pride happens when we transmute religious realities into fuel for the polishing of egos—the honours we accumulate, the creation of hierarchies, the accumulation of titles, the deference we attract. The humble way of Christ is thus hijacked, becoming a device for self-advancement or self-promotion. This is a long way from the way of Christ.

No doubt Jesus is using an element of hyperbole in verses 8–10 (should we not call our fathers 'father'?) but it is difficult to escape the impression that he intended the community of his followers to be as non-hierarchical as it is possible to be, a community of equals and servants who have forsaken self-promotion and pride (v. 11). It is also hard not to conclude that his church has largely ignored what he had to say.

4 More things to avoid

Jesus' breach with the Pharisees seems to be made complete by the words he utters against them here. If the church is given the keys that enable it to open the door of the kingdom of heaven to those as yet outside (16:19), the Pharisees by contrast lock people out of the kingdom (v. 13). Although they are strenuous in seeking converts, those converts are the wrong kind: the Pharisees are converting other Jewish believers to their own party and mindset rather than from unbelief to belief. The result is simply more of the same mistaken thinking (v. 15).

Four times in these verses (and again in verse 26) Jesus accuses the Pharisees of being blind. He is standing in front of them as the one who has come from God with power to heal and to bless, a sight that precious few have been privileged to behold, and yet he goes unrecognised. This is indeed spiritual blindness (John 3:3) and, as a result, they lead people astray. They cannot see the kingdom of God as it has dawned in Christ. Instead they concentrate on minute issues of practice while missing what really matters. Jesus is not indifferent to those lesser matters, just aware of their capacity to deflect attention from the primary concerns of justice, mercy and faith that are at the core of Hebrew religion (v. 23). The image of straining out a gnat and swallowing a camel (v. 24) is characteristic of Jesus' rhetoric (and sarcasm). A devout Pharisee would strain water through a cloth to avoid swallowing a gnat, one of the smallest of unclean animals. But a camel, one of the largest, they allow to pass unnoticed.

In the history of the Christian church, parallels to the Pharisees are far from uncommon. It is healthier when devout people seek to inhabit the centre ground of Christian belief and practice rather than becoming obsessed with esoteric and minor doctrines, unprofitable speculation or variations of practice. 'In essentials unity, in non-essentials diversity, and in all things charity' is a good principle to follow. It is not wrong to have personal opinions, but it is unproductive when they cause us to lose sight of what is at the centre. The Pharisees were blind to Jesus himself as God's Son and the world's Messiah.

5 A history of disobedience

Frequently we might notice how the Gospels uncover the shortcomings of the early church's leading characters, who are portrayed not romantically but 'warts and all'. In this respect the Gospels follow the Old Testament, which is every bit as relentless as Jesus in exposing the ways in which Israel went wrong. There is nothing anti-Jewish here, just an intra-Jewish critique of the nation's failures.

In this section of Matthew's Gospel there is a convergence of perspective as Jesus places the Pharisees of his day in continuity with those who, in the past, rejected and ill-treated God's servants. They are about to do again what they have always done (vv. 29–36). Although these Pharisees and, no doubt, others might have rehearsed Israel's history and always put themselves in the place of the 'good guys' (v. 30), Jesus exposes them. They are doing what their ancestors did, and worse (v. 31). However good they look on the outside, the reality is that they are inwardly corrupt (vv. 27–28). They are liable to divine judgement and will not escape (vv. 38–39).

Of the things Jesus was unwilling to tolerate, hypocrisy was high on the list. Hypocrisy is about acting a part, pretending to be on the outside something that we are not on the inside. What is on the inside, the reality of what we are, was very important to Jesus (v. 25). It should be equally important to us. We all face the temptation to fit in with whatever groups we belong to, not to be different from others. This can lead to an outward conformity to the Christian community that is a bit like playing a part. It is the start of a slippery slope.

Truth to tell, it is hard not to be a little hypocritical, but this does not justify it. All of us aspire to be something we are not yet, and this leaves a gap between aspiration and achievement. We carry a name, 'Christian', of which we were never worthy in the first place and are likely never to deserve. We could feel condemned, but this would not help. Better to be simply honest and to confess, 'I am not what I should be. I am not what I could be. But I am not what I was, and by the grace of God I am what I am' (attributed to John Newton).

6 Jerusalem, Jerusalem

Matthew 23:37–39

It is with immense relief that we now encounter these tender words of Jesus—relief, because most of the preceding chapter has been fierce and judgemental. Jesus has not spared the Pharisees, nor by derivation their descendants in the church. Of course, he is qualified to pass this judgement, but now we perceive him in different mode. He grieves over the city. The traditional location for the utterance of these words is on the Mount of Olives, overlooking the Temple Mount. This is credible, since it was on the route to and from Bethany, where Jesus habitually stayed, and is mentioned specifically in 24:3. There is a moving and striking view of the Temple Mount from this vantage point.

Today, at this location, there is also a small chapel in the shape of a tear. In AD70 it would have been the place where the Roman tenth legion encamped as it laid siege to the city, before destroying it and breaking down the temple stone by stone, leaving it desolate.

Jesus yearns over Jerusalem and its ambiguous history (v. 37). The image is a maternal one: it recalls the mother hen gathering her chicks under her wings to protect and shelter them. Beyond all the fierce words he has uttered, this is what Jesus sought repeatedly to do. Now things have reached their conclusion. Christ and his peaceful way have been met with unwillingness and stubborn rejection, and events are moving to their climax.

There is a profoundly significant picture here of the God who comes seeking after those who are lost, in order to save them. He comes to us too, in our time and in our place. Jesus was accompanied by his disciples, so it is clear that not all in Israel rejected him. There was a community of disciples, but even so, the majority had not welcomed him. He had come to his own, but his own had not received him or believed in his name (John 1:11–12). In like manner, we might imagine that Christ yearns over all creation, that he comes to heal and save and, to do so, draws near by the Spirit. The chapters we have read are a crucial part of that drawing near. How we respond to them is for us to decide, but Jesus deserves the best that we can bring him.

Guidelines

'For many are called, but few are chosen.' What do these words, which we encounter in Matthew 22:14, actually mean? Those who place a strong emphasis on divine sovereignty read them as saying, 'The message of Christ goes out to all, but in the end it is God's purpose to choose for himself only some and not all.' The ones who are truly chosen respond to the call of God in repentance and faith and show themselves to be Christ's disciples. Other commentators find them offering a similar perspective to that of the parable of the sower (Matthew 13:1–9). The word of God is widely preached and all are freely called into the kingdom, but not all enter in. There is a rate of attrition: only a minority realise the possibility of being among God's chosen people.

The reality of Jesus' experience could correspond to either reading. As he began his ministry, large crowds gathered to hear him, to be set free or healed of their ailments. Jesus achieved a popularity that alarmed and upset the established order, but, as his ministry progressed and hostility intensified, so the crowds were reduced. As he approached the end of his mission, he was abandoned by many, including, for a time, the very disciples he had trained and whom he had several times warned of what was about to happen.

Following Jesus was not and is not easy. It is a journey to the cross of personal self-denial, losing oneself in order to find oneself. It is a call to be different from other people. There have been times and places when following Jesus has been immensely popular, and times and places when the opposite has been the case. Nobody ever said such a journey would be easy. But there is also a joy in placing one's trust in such an extraordinary human being, whose name is above every other name, and venturing all on the informed probability that he is exactly who he thought he was.

If we are looking for something that is morally and personally demanding, if we are dissatisfied with what passes in popular culture as the good life, and if we think there must be something greater and better than anything else on offer in the world, then the way of Christ is surely it. He is our reference-point, our example and our power for living.

Amos

Amos is a very important book of the Bible, for a number of reasons. Although it is quite slight in length, in comparison with Isaiah, Jeremiah or Ezekiel, its significance is great. It is almost hidden away among the 'Book of the Twelve' or the 'minor prophets', as they are frequently called in English, but none of this detracts from its importance.

Amos was the earliest of the 'writing prophets'. He probably delivered his message between 760 and 750BC. Although we know a lot about the mission of other prophets, like Elijah and Elisha, who came earlier in history, we do not have collections of their 'words', so we lack any sense of their theology or even their style. We do have some of the words of Nathan, the prophet who addressed David, but their focus is quite specific and lacks the comprehensiveness that we find with Amos—addressing all Israel, whether the ten tribes or the twelve.

With Amos we find that in many ways his style is characteristic of the writing prophets. We see his passionate concern for social justice and his conflict with the royal priests and their sanctuaries, challenging the view that religious ritual was enough to satisfy the God of the covenant. We hear his powerful words and idioms, often spoken in the first person singular on behalf of 'the Lord'. We get glimpses into the prophetic calling and the awareness that God does nothing without revealing it to his prophets. We find here a strong sense of the visual aspect of revelation as well as the verbal. There is a predilection for wordplay, as though words themselves have some inherent power.

But Amos is no narrow religious fanatic. Although, unlike Isaiah and Jeremiah, he does not have access to the king, he does have a keen awareness of political, economic and social issues. He is thoroughly immersed in his own culture, as his use of wisdom sayings and perspectives illustrates. He certainly knows how to engage his varied audiences, as we shall see. But always, he speaks for God.

Quotations are taken from the New Revised Standard Version.

1 The lion's roar

Amos 1:2—2:5

The opening words of Amos's prophecy are 'The Lord roars from Zion ...'. These certainly set the tone for the opening salvo of thunderous denunciations. As a 'shepherd', just like the boy David, Amos would have experienced and remembered the terror that the roar of the lion, echoing across the valley, would strike into sheep and shepherd too. Before the terror from one roar had died down, another would follow.

Here, then, we have a number of roars—against the Syrians (Damascus), the Philistines (Gaza, Ashdod, Ashkelon and Ekron), Tyre, Edom (Teman and Bozrah), the Ammonites (Rabbah) and Moab (Kerioth), making six in all. Each has a very similar structure. 'Thus says the Lord...' is the 'messenger formula'—fitting for prophets who are messengers of Yahweh, the great superpower initiating a suzerain treaty. Next, the phrase 'For three transgressions... and for four' indicates the reason for the judgement, along with the strong statement, 'I will not revoke the punishment.' Then comes a usually short statement of the accusation, with, finally, a more extended announcement of the punishment.

Many of the larger collections of prophecy contain 'oracles against the nations', but those oracles often come towards the end of the book, or at least at the end of a section. Amos, however, begins with them, and this is certainly an attention-grabbing start. His oracles indicate that Amos, while claiming to be a rather ordinary person, not from the ruling elite in Jerusalem, had an amazing political awareness. There were no newspapers or TV news reports, but he knew a lot.

If this is extraordinary, what follows is staggering. Often, the 'oracles against the nations' are followed by promises of salvation for Israel; the destruction of enemies is a prelude to Israel's rescue. But here it is the opposite. Just as Amos's hearers are about to burst into applause, 'Thus says the Lord: For three transgressions of Judah, and for four, I will not revoke the punishment' (2:4).

The reason is serious: 'They have rejected the law of the Lord'. In other words, they have broken their covenant agreement with Yahweh. Hence, the fitting punishment is 'fire on Judah' and the devastation of Jerusalem.

Thus the seventh 'oracle against the nations' is turned on its head—against the city that prided itself on being the crown jewel of Yahweh.

2 Enigma variations

Amos 2:6–16

This passage brings into focus one of the enigmas of the book of Amos. We will explore the enigma by considering the overall structure of this opening section of 'oracles against the nations'. Structurally, the previous section was complete—six oracles against the other nations, then one against Judah (like the six days of creation and one day of rest). All the oracles were of a similar length, too. Now, however, we are faced with a much longer oracle against Israel. It begins with the same introduction as the other seven ('Thus says the Lord: For three… and for four…') but is then expanded. In fact, we don't get to the 'pronouncement of judgement' until 2:13.

Although Amos directs some of the rest of his book to Zion/Jerusalem and Judah (for example, 6:1) and he is aware of traditions associated with David (6:5), his main focus is the ten northern tribes of Israel. Samaria, Bethel, Gilgal and Beersheba are the areas named. So here is the enigma: is the oracle against Judah (2:4–5) a later insertion, to give the whole book a new application to Jerusalem and Judah—perhaps after Amos's prophecies have been vindicated by the Assyrian sack of Samaria? Or, assuming that he is addressing a northern audience (7:10), does the oracle against Judah have the same function as the previous six—heightening the impact of the judgement on Israel? This issue emerges in other parts of the book too.

What is clear from 2:6–16 is the penetration of Amos's critical insights against Israel. Again, there is a marked contrast with the first six, where the criticisms related to their military oppression of other nations. With Israel, the criticisms are all concerned with internal wrongs. There are three main issues. The first accusation is of oppression of the poor (vv. 6–7a) and probably relates to some kind of slavery, although it might be about judges being bribed to deliver verdicts against the poor. The second suggests a distortion of Yahweh worship into a syncretistic kind of Baal worship (vv. 7b–8), although it might be more about breaking sexual taboos. The third is about the contamination of the Nazirites and prophets that God had raised up (vv. 10–12), neutralising the people appointed by God to call other Israelites to a holy life.

3 The lion has roared

In verse 4, we are asked, 'Does a lion roar in the forest, when it has no prey?' This illustrates several things for us about Amos's message. First, we can see from verses 3–6 that Amos is a skilful orator. He brings together a series of metaphors that increase the demand on the attention of the hearers (there are six or seven such rhetorical questions). They are taken from many areas of life, including human social conduct, violent animals, birds caught in a trap, and the warning siren of a trumpet being sounded in the city. In this respect, Amos's method can be considered similar to Wisdom approaches (see Clements, *Prophecy and Tradition*, p. 77), although its message is far more subtle and penetrating.

Second, therefore, we note the way the series of pictures begins and ends. It starts by referring to two people who have made an appointment to meet and travel together (3:2). This picks up from Amos's opening words. In verse 1 he recalls the great exodus tradition that is the foundation for his understanding of Israel's relationship with God. Israel is the family that God has brought up from Egypt. Hence, God has been walking from Egypt with Israel until now. But now the question is being raised: what happens when they no longer have 'an appointment'?

The series ends with what might have been a proverbial saying: 'Does disaster befall a city, unless the Lord has done it?' Yet, this brings us face to face with the judgement. Amos is going to speak of judgement against the city of Samaria (the political capital of the ten northern tribes) in 3:9–11 and Bethel (the religious capital where Israel went for its 'appointments' during the festivals) in verses 13–15.

Finally, we are given insights into Amos's understanding of the prophet's role, in verses 7–8. He is aware of a group of prophets (he refers to them in the plural), but it is unclear whether he is thinking of a contemporary collective, of which he was a part, or of a prophetic succession over time. What is clear is that they are Yahweh's servants and are therefore bound to do as they are commanded. Also, it is probably implied that their key task is to deliver God's message to those who have broken the covenant with him (v. 8).

4 The appointment at Bethel

Amos 4:4–13

Bethel has already been singled out for judgment in 3:14: 'On the day I punish Israel for its transgressions, I will punish the altars of Bethel.' We can speculate as to whether this indicates that the punishment of Israel will begin with Bethel or whether the emphasis is on the fact that not even Bethel (the appointed sanctuary, as it was viewed in Israel) will escape. Now we hear of the reason why Bethel and Gilgal (another sacred site) will not escape God's judgement.

The appeal in verse 4 ('Come to Bethel… to Gilgal') echoes the invitation from the priests, on behalf of God, to participate in the divinely appointed festivals. This provided the opportunity for Israel to renew her relationship with God through various sacrifices (see, for example, Leviticus 1—4; Deuteronomy 16). But Amos treats all of this with total irony. In going to the sacred cities, they were rebelling and transgressing. Israel offered her sacrifices not to please God or in obedience to him and reverence for him, but for her own satisfaction.

Participation in the worship at the sacred places should have brought restoration and prosperity. What follows, however, is a litany of disasters. It is significant that they are described as coming from God: the use of the first person singular and the directness of the address are reinforced by the phrase 'says the Lord', ensuring that there is no room for ambivalence. Like a drum beat, this phrase recurs. The 'plagues' are reminiscent of the plagues against Egypt; indeed, this point is underlined in verse 10. But the other part of the refrain is 'Yet you did not return to me' (vv. 6, 8, 9, 10, 11). The purpose of these 'punishments' was restorative, but Israel took no notice of the warnings.

Now, however, the period of attempted recall is over. The call of God through various warning events now becomes the ground for his judgement: '*Therefore*… prepare to meet your God, O Israel' (v. 12, my emphasis).

Meeting with God and experiencing his gracious encouragement and deliverance were at the heart of the sacrificial system, but now this purpose too is reversed. Instead of being a meeting of deliverance, it becomes the ultimate threat.

5 The last chance?

This passage begins with a dreadful lamentation—presumably by God over the ten northern tribes, the 'house of Israel'. Israel is pictured as a beautiful young woman who should be getting ready for her wedding day. Instead, she has been beaten to the ground and there is no one to rescue her, even if she calls out for help (see Deuteronomy 22:25–27). As a lamentation, it should indicate that the fate described has already taken place. This is the outcome of God's summons to her to meet him for judgment (4:12)—a devastating and total punishment. The metaphor is then 'translated' in terms of the destruction of the people (who are seeking to flee) or the armies (that went from the cities to fight). They are reduced to a tenth of their original number.

Yet, other verses indicate that the verdict has not yet been pronounced and the punishment not yet implemented: 'Seek me and live...' (vv. 4, 6); 'Seek good and not evil, that you may live' (v. 14).

It is also clear that there was a strong tendency to complacency among the people. The Israelites were enjoying relative prosperity (at least, the powerful were). They had built their houses with hewn stone—material usually utilised only for temples and palaces. They had planted vineyards—an indication of stability and peace (v. 11). They may have been keen enough to worship at their sanctuaries (Bethel, Gilgal and Beersheba), but, in so doing, they were not 'seeking the Lord' but were seeking their own satisfaction and pleasure. The evidence for this claim is that they were corrupting justice and not upholding it as God's covenant required (v. 7). They were abusing or silencing those who attempted to uphold the justice system (vv. 10, 12) and they were crushing the poor and stealing from them the little they had managed to grow (v. 11).

What they fail to realise is that God is the supreme judge. They cannot distort the truth or bribe him. He knows their behaviour and names it 'transgressions' and 'sins' (v. 12). So the Lord will pass through their midst, as the angel of death did to the Egyptians—unless they 'seek good and not evil... Hate evil and love good, and establish justice in the gate' (vv. 14–15).

6 The Day of the Lord

We have heard the roar of the lion in Amos 1:2. We have been taken into the psyche of this terrifying animal in 3:4, and now we learn that there is something worse—the message of judgement from God. Verse 19 tells us it is like meeting a bear, from which there is no escape. As people have tried to ignore the potentially destructive judgement of God, they are now about to face his reality—the day of the Lord.

The 'day of the Lord' should mean a day in which God acts decisively to destroy Israel's enemies. The day of the Lord was the time when God brought deliverance by destroying those who stood in his (and Israel's) way. So it became synonymous with a time for celebrating the release from all danger and into freedom. It would be a day for praising God—the dawn after the darkness.

Not so, says Amos! It will be darkness and gloom, not light. It may promise respite and relaxation—but beware! As you lean against the wall, a poisonous snake bites. Just as you think you've eluded the lion, you come face to face with a bear. This means that the Israelites are, in fact, God's enemy. He has turned against them.

It was in Israel's festivals that they celebrated the 'days of the Lord'—especially their deliverance from Egypt and entry into the land of promise. So God ought surely to be pleased with Israel for keeping up these festivals. Yet, at the very moment when these festivals are brought into the picture, God speaks condemnation. The festivals were meant to ensure Israel's security, to bind God to looking after them, but here he says, 'I hate, I despise your festivals… Take away from me the noise of your songs' (vv. 21, 23). God's verdict is that he will not accept their sacrifices.

Here is something appalling. It is hard to over-emphasise the shock of these words. The religious rituals were assumed to be the mechanism by which Israel's relationship with God was sustained. Yet, along with many other prophets, Amos brings God's message that the proper procedures without the integrity that they require leads to disaster, not prosperity. Perhaps the most memorable of all his words are these: 'But let justice roll down like waters, and righteousness like an ever-flowing stream' (v. 24).

Guidelines

In many ways and on many occasions, Amos can relate his message to the culture around him, indicating a keen sense of political awareness. How important is it for us, as Christian people with a prophetic message for our society, that we are culturally aware? How do you seek to keep alert? By reading a newspaper, watching one or more 'soaps', listening regularly to the news, or engaging on Twitter with those who are culturally alert?

What else do we need to do or be if God is to use us to challenge and correct the culture in which we live? Who do you think has been used in this way?

Pray for people like the Archbishop of Canterbury and the Pope, who have special opportunities on national and international platforms.

How can we avoid the perennial danger for people who are involved in religious life, institutions and activities of coming to believe that these activities are an end in themselves? They become empty if they do not translate into personal and societal integrity and justice.

3–9 July

1 The complacency of capital cities

Amos 6:1–7

As we begin our second week with Amos, we notice an emphasis on 'all Israel': 'Alas for those who are at ease in Zion, and for those who feel secure on Mount Samaria' (v. 1). By this time, the united kingdom of Solomon had split into two parts—Judah in the south, with its political, economic and religious capital in Jerusalem (or Zion), and the ten northern tribes of Israel, whose political capital was Samaria. At this time (unlike the time of Jesus: see John 4:19–21), Israel's religious centres of worship were Bethel and, initially, Dan (see 1 Kings 12:28–30). However, Amos probably has in his sights the economic and political centres rather than the religious centres. Hence, the focus of his critique here is not the corruption of worship but the improper acquisitions that come with affluence.

There are two sections beginning with 'Alas' (vv. 1, 4), but their contents are very different. The first is more political, the second more social in its focus. In verses 1–3, a challenge is made by reference to other nation or city states. These places had once been renowned for their power and security, but their present defeated status told a different story. Amos's point is that history indicates that Israel and Zion should not count on their current prosperity and power as any kind of guarantee for the future.

Verses 4–7 indicate a moral disease that warrants divine judgement. Perhaps this section depicts a single scene—something like a banquet—where guests are lounging about, having the most luxurious food and drink, singing songs or being entertained and indulging themselves with wine and perfume; or perhaps each of these activities should be taken as a separate and distinct criticism. There is no direct mention of sexual immorality, depravity or violence against others. The critical point, however, is not the indulgence but the fact that it is enjoyed without any regard for those who suffer: the revellers 'are not grieved over the ruin of Joseph' (v. 6). The rich man has no awareness of Lazarus at his gate!

The judgement is that such revelry is about to end. It is these very people, complacent in their affluence and superiority. who will be taken into exile. This was clearly the case with the deportation of Judah's elite during the Babylonian exile, but the application is not so clear regarding the northern kingdom.

2 The real price of victory

Amos 6:8–14

God abhors 'the pride of Jacob' (v. 8). This could mean that God detests the object of Jacob's pride—possibly one of the religious centres or, more likely, one of the cities mentioned in 6:1, either Zion or Samaria. The following line, about hating 'his strongholds', suggests that the latter is the correct understanding, as does the indication that the city will be ransacked and its inhabitants delivered up (presumably, to an invading army). This idea is reinforced by the punishment described in verse 11. Often, references to 'Jacob' are understood as referring to the northern tribes, but there are also signs that the 'God of Jacob' was associated with Zion and the Jerusalem temple (for example, Psalms 46 and 76).

Verses 13–14 recognise a different kind of pride—the pride of those who have been victorious in battle. Because of the weakness of Damascus, crippled by Assyrian pressure, Jeroboam II had been able to reclaim Israel's previous losses (see 2 Kings 14:25–28). Lo-debar (mentioned in 2

Samuel 9:4-5), located in the eastern part of Gilead, was one of the cities recaptured. Amos, however, mocks this military self-satisfaction by calling the city Lo-dabar, which means 'nothing'. (This detail is clear in the Hebrew but is not apparent in the NRSV.) Amos, as we have seen, enjoys playing with words—but this was probably viewed as very serious play. Through the pun, Amos robs the city of its significance. In fact, it was probably the name's susceptibility to wordplay that prompted Amos to select this city as his example, rather than others he could have chosen. The ease of the pun reflects the vulnerability of the city to having its military success overturned.

The emphasis on 'our own strength' (v. 13) underlines the pride that Israel's leaders are taking in their success, but the punishment indicates their total vulnerability. Yahweh is going to empower another nation to harass them throughout the length and breadth of Jeroboam II's territory (which is what the phrase 'from Lebo-hamath to the Wadi Arabah' signifies).

Verse 12 indicates that Israel has completely reversed the 'natural order' within the covenant of faith. The 'wisdom-like' questions imply the unnaturalness of what they have done. So God's action, countering their attitudes or actions with the opposite outcome, is ironically natural, or justified, given the circumstances.

3 The real cost to Amos

Amos 7:1–9

At this point in the prophetic collection we can note a change. Rather than hearing the prophet speaking out God's word (though clearly shaped by his own impressively broad historical, religious and cultural awareness), we now start to engage much more with Amos himself. The messages that we have heard may seem harsh, almost as though Amos enjoyed delivering God's verdict of condemnation and destruction—as the Rabshakeh seemed to enjoy bringing the Assyrian king's message to Jerusalem (see 2 Kings 18:19–35). After all, Amos was the Lord's messenger, just as the Rabshakeh was Sennacherib's. But from now on we can enter into the various struggles that it brought for Amos.

First we see that Amos had interceded time and time again, seeking to avert God's destructive judgement. We are given two cameos—locusts with an unquenchable appetite and fire with its insatiable power of destruction.

Both are completely beyond human capacity to mitigate; both can only be endured. With each vision, Amos pleads with God and God relents.

These cameos indicate one of the modes of God's communication with Amos: 'the Lord God showed me'. There is a strong visual element to his encounters with God. They also underline one of the key roles of the prophet—to take the risk of pleading for others before God. Notice how all of this is directed against 'Jacob', as well as how, in contrast to the nation's own sense of aggrandisement, Amos sees Jacob as 'so small'.

The punishment specifies the destruction of the centres of worship (v. 9) as well as the 'house of Jeroboam'. The two pillars of Israelite society—the monarchy (thus political, economic and military leadership) and the religious centres, through which the covenant was restored both for the individuals and the nation—will be destroyed. The house of Jacob will collapse.

4 Religious conflicts

Amos 7:10–17

This passage is full of conflicts; it is also a very significant passage, for several reasons. At the heart of it seems to be a conflict between two aspects of Israel's religion—the priestly and the prophetic. Amaziah was presumably the 'high priest' at Bethel, and, because Bethel was 'the king's sanctuary' and 'a temple of the kingdom' (v. 13), he owed allegiance to the king and the kingdom. Amaziah sees Amos as an upstart from Judah—a prophetic terrorist, using his divine powers to plant seeds of destruction in Israel—so he reports Amos to King Jeroboam for starting a 'conspiracy'. But he also sees Amos as under some kind of economic tutelage; this is the implication of verse 12. Presumably he suspects that Amos has been sent from the south to damage the north.

However, Amaziah shows personal courage in confronting Amos directly. It was a risky thing to do: see Amos's judgement on Amaziah in verses 16–17. So it may not be completely accurate to perceive this conflict simply as a priestly–prophetic issue. Prophets could be paid by the king too. There could be faithful priests and unfaithful prophets. There could certainly be conflict between rival prophets and rival priests, all concerned for the safety of their people, including the struggle for true faith in Yahweh.

A second reason why this is a significant passage is for the insight it gives us into Amos's call as a prophet and the nature of prophecy. Initially Amos deals with the accusation that he is being paid for his work: he is not a professional prophet (v. 14). The phrase 'nor a prophet's son' suggests that the role of prophecy could be inherited—unless 'prophet's son' is to be taken in the sense that Hebrew uses 'son of…' to describe a similar characteristic rather than a familial relationship. Then he claims that 'the Lord took me…' (v. 15). He was not invited to the role; God insisted on it. He also counters the claim that he is a 'foreigner' from Judah, saying that God told him, 'Go, prophesy to my people Israel.' However, this may be more than a simple political demarcation; Amos may be claiming that he is sent to all twelve tribes or, indeed, that only this divine concept of Israel (the twelve tribes in unity) has validity, not the political entity carved out by Jeroboam.

5 The deep and dangerous famine

Amos 8:1–14

The opening words of verse 1, 'This is what the Lord God showed me', in sequence with 7:1, 4 and 7, might suggest that 7:10–17 is some kind of 'insertion' into a series of visions. This does not necessarily mean, though, that it was an inappropriate interjection. Indeed, it may have been used to heighten the justification for God's decision to break off completely his relationship with the northern tribes and to emphasise the inevitability of the outcome.

In the section beginning at verse 4, which breaks the series of visions, we have some of Amos's clearest denunciations of the moral evil of using political and economic power to oppress the poor. God's oath on 'the pride of Jacob' (v. 7) picks up on 6:8, raising the possibility that we have here some kind of chiasmic structure. If so, the central element (and therefore the one on which most attention is focused) is the conflict between Amos and Amaziah.

We then return to the theme of 'On that day' (v. 9), which relates conceptually to 5:18. As there, so here, there is a sense of 'reversal'. The 'Day of the Lord' may well have been celebrated in the temple with songs (v. 3) and feasts (v. 10), as indicated by psalms such as 96—99. But such celebrations will be short-lived. Indeed, at the heart of those psalms is a sense that God comes to uphold and establish justice (see Psalm 96:13; 97:10–12; 98:9). Through Amos, God is demanding true social justice, not the feasting of those who claim to be God's people. Their songs will become wailings and lamentation.

Often among the prophets, including Amos, God's judgement is seen in terms of military oppression and its consequences—commonly death, humiliation and starvation. Now, however, a new element appears—a famine, but this time of the word of the Lord (vv. 11–12). The people have attempted to silence the prophets (2:11–12); Amaziah has done his best to silence Amos (7:12–13). So the outcome is that there is no word from God through his prophets when the people seek it. They look for an 'oracle of salvation'—a word from God announcing that the punishment is over (as in Isaiah 40)—but it is not forthcoming. The punishment fits the crime.

6 How will it end?

Amos 9:1–15

Sometimes novels are provided with alternative endings, so that the reader can choose their own. This concluding chapter of Amos appears rather similar: verses 1–10 describe catastrophic gloom; verses 11–15 depict glorious salvation.

When Amos writes, 'I saw the Lord standing beside the altar' (v. 1), is he referring to an altar in an earthly temple, such as Bethel, or the altar in heaven (as in Isaiah 6:6)? The prophet's words 'I saw…' appear to echo Isaiah 6:1. However, God's command to shake the pillars so that they fall on people implies an earthly temple—unless it is to be understood like the visions in Revelation, where heavenly events have earthly repercussions. We will never be sure, but what is clear is the total and devastating judgement of Israel by God. His 'chosen' people are no more chosen than other nations, including the despised Philistines (v. 7).

Verse 8 begins, 'The eyes of the Lord God are upon the sinful kingdom, and I will destroy it from the face of the earth.' Yet, as so often in Amos, what seems categorical turns out to be less so: the verse continues, '… except that I will not utterly destroy the house of Jacob.' Verses 9–10 continue the theme of divine judgement with a sword that God himself wields. But maybe the image of the sieve implies some kind of remnant (the pebbles that don't fall). Certainly the next sections emphasise restoration: 'On that day I will raise up the booth of David that is fallen' (v. 11).

We are never quite sure of the extent of the intended judgement. Does 'house of Jacob' (v. 8) mean the twelve tribes, including Judah (for Jacob's household included all twelve tribes: see Genesis 49), or only the ten northern ones? Does 'David's booth' refer only to Judah or the temple itself (see 2 Samuel 7:1–16) or to the whole kingdom? Verses 14–15 suggest the restoration of all Israel to the whole land.

Perhaps we can make sense of the oscillation between total warranted destruction and the promise of restoration along these lines: Israel (whether the ten tribes or the twelve) *deserve* total condemnation and extermination, but God never implements this judgement completely because to do so would mean that his purposes have been completely thwarted. In some ways, Paul wrestles with the same tensions in Romans 9—11.

Guidelines

On occasions, Amos seeks to undermine any sense of 'special privilege' for the people of God. In what ways do you think it is helpful for Christians to think of themselves as special, 'the chosen people', and in what ways can it be dangerous? Think of specific, concrete examples if you can.

Amos goes as far as claiming that Israel's special rescue from Egypt by God is no different from the rescue of other nations (9:7). Although Amos intended this to undermine Israel's complacency, do you think it is legitimate to glimpse here God's love for 'the whole world' (John 3:16)?

Amos indicates that the ultimate punishment may well be that of a famine 'of hearing the words of the Lord' (8:11–12). Other scriptures also imply that hearing from God is more important even than having food or water (Deuteronomy 8:3; John 6:35–51). Try to imagine what this is saying about hearing from God. In the light of this, ask yourself whether we value enough (a) the Bible, (b) those who help us hear from God, and (c) our own relationship with God.

FURTHER READING

R.E. Clements, *Prophecy and Tradition*, Blackwell, 1975.

J.L. Mays, *Amos*, SCM, 1969.

H. Mowvley, *The Books of Amos and Hosea*, Epworth, 1991 (pp. 1–91).

D. Stuart, *Hosea to Jonah* (Word Biblical Commentary 31), Zondervan, 2014, pp. 273–400.

H.W. Wolff, *Amos the Prophet: The man and his background*, Fortress, 1973.

Discipleship today

In recent years, much thinking has been done about what discipleship means, and how we help one another to become more effective disciples. As numbers of people associating themselves with churches have continued to fall nationally, we seem to have realised that quality as well as quantity counts.

In the first week of the following notes, we shall be looking at the Gospels to discover exactly what Jesus called his disciples to do. We shall explore a six-stage process of discipleship: Come – Follow – Leave – Learn – Change – Go. Each Bible passage will help us to reflect on what this process might mean for us today, and encourage us to see ourselves as being on that same journey.

Of course, being a disciple in first-century Palestine is not the same as living a life of discipleship today. Following Jesus is never easy, but each time and place brings its own set of issues. Where I live in England we are not, at the moment, likely to be martyred if we confess the name of Christ, but that doesn't mean there are no pressures on us to deny or simply to compromise our faith. So, in the second week of readings we shall be looking at some contemporary factors that can subtly gnaw at discipleship, making us weak and ineffective as Christians and damaging God's reputation and that of his church. Our issues tend to be subtler and more complex than the simple question of whether or not to burn incense to the Emperor to honour his deity. But they are just as significant, and need as robust a resistance as ever.

Fortunately we do not fight alone against these subtle pressures to conform. God's Spirit is the same Spirit who caused the early Christians to proclaim, in the face of death, 'Jesus is Lord!' God's word contains principles that speak to our situations as clearly as they ever did. Christ continues to give to his church teachers to help us understand the world around us from God's perspective and apply God's word to our lives.

One important weapon in our fight is what the Bible calls 'wisdom'. Wisdom is not about being clever or academic: it is much closer to the French term *savoir faire*, literally 'knowing what to do'. By taking a good look at some of today's issues, we can understand how insidious they are, and how we might best resist them through knowledge of the word and the power of the Spirit.

1 Come

Mark 3:7–19

It is as though the Bible passages for this week have a pair of brackets around them: 'Come' and 'Go'. In fact, Jesus' purpose according to Mark reflects that pattern exactly: his disciples were called to come to him, to be with him, and then to be sent out from him (vv. 13–14). But we begin with that calling to 'come'. It is significant that, here in Mark and also in Luke's accounts of the calling of his first disciples, Jesus has been ministering to large crowds, but then selects from them individuals whom he specifically calls (see Luke 5—6). Of course it is not that he wasn't interested in the others, but he must have sensed in his spirit some individuals who seemed particularly appropriate to be members of his closest group.

You are, I'm sure, reading this today because you see yourself as someone on the journey of discipleship. It will be encouraging as we start these readings to think of ourselves as those whom Jesus has called, first and foremost, to come to him, to be with him. At some point we encountered Jesus, perhaps through the example of family or friends, or maybe as a result of a process of drawing near to God, or even a 'Damascus road' experience. But what matters is that we have responded to Jesus' call and have, in some way, come to him. This has not happened randomly: Jesus himself has called us, and the path of discipleship has opened up because we chose to respond, and, with that single step, to begin a lifelong journey with him.

You might like to reflect today on how you have felt Jesus' call to come to him, and what it has meant to you so far. You may also like to think about what 'being with Jesus' means for you, and how that is similar to, yet different from, what it meant for the disciples named by Mark.

It is possible, of course, that you are not yet sure that you have started the discipleship journey: you are still weighing up the consequences of coming to Christ. Perhaps this week you will feel ready to begin to walk his way, a walk that can only begin when we first come to him.

2 Follow

Coming to Jesus is an essential first step in discipleship, but it is only the first step. In today's passage we see various people beginning to follow him. John the Baptist's disciples take the word literally, walking away from John and physically following after Jesus as he passes by.

For Jesus' first disciples, following him did indeed involve physical travel, with an itinerant ministry first in Galilee and then in Jerusalem. But there is more to following than just walking around. We 'follow' a band or football team: they become important to us, perhaps even an obsession. We 'follow' a route that will take us to our destination. We 'follow' a particular school of thought or behaviour, such that our whole lives are shaped by it. We 'follow' a course of learning or a career path, becoming more and more proficient at it. And we 'follow' the example of an older and wiser exponent: as I write, my son has just bought his first house and is putting into practice all those DIY skills on which he has worked with me in the past.

Following Jesus as his disciple means all of the above and more. All these ways of understanding the idea of following are dynamic: they involve some kind of growth or journey. Above all, though, discipleship is about following Jesus' example and becoming more and more like him. We go where Jesus would go, do what he would do, react to different situations as he would react, treat others as he would treat them, and so on. We imitate him, in order to become more and more like him.

I am constantly challenged by passages such as 1 Corinthians 4:16, where Paul encourages the members of his churches to imitate him. I would never have the nerve to say to the congregations among whom I have served, 'If you want to be a true Christian, just do exactly what you have seen me doing'! Yet Paul doesn't baulk at the idea, because, as a disciple himself, he has learnt what it means to imitate Christ.

3 Leave

In my experience, this aspect of discipleship—leaving—is the one least talked about in Christian circles, and least mentioned in our evangelism.

Jesus' first followers discovered that coming to him and following him meant leaving some other things behind. For the fishermen in today's passage, it was their boats and their nets, which stood for their previous careers, livelihood and security. For Levi it meant leaving his financial greed, for Zacchaeus his dishonesty, for an immoral woman her sexual sin. I sometimes wonder whether, in our proclamation of the Christian gospel, we have become reluctant to spell out the fact that, for many of Jesus' followers, there had to be a clean break with the past.

We see the same idea earlier in the Bible. In Genesis 12:1, God calls Abram, and is very specific about what he is to leave (his country, his people, his father's household) and extremely vague about where he is going ('the land I will show you'). Following Jesus can be similar, and, as we set off, the sacrifices we make can appear far more significant than the rewards we hope to gain.

That is why many disciples today travel, as it were, with their nets on their back, pulling their boats or their money-sacks along after them. No wonder progress can be slow! We are not good at helping people to leave behind the things that keep them anchored in their pre-Christian lives, things that perhaps provided security or even livelihood for them. Of course, Paul advises against radical changes of status (1 Corinthians 7:17–24), yet disciples can still carry unhelpful baggage from the past.

What has being a disciple of Jesus cost you? What have you had to leave behind in order to come to him and follow him, and what has not had to change? To use another of Jesus' pictures, what have you had to sell in order to buy the priceless pearl of discipleship? And have you had value for money? Some days you will probably feel more positive than others about the things you have had to leave. Some days you will look forward with hope: other days you will look back with disappointment or even regret. But we do people a disservice if we suggest that nothing has to go, to make room for Jesus in their lives.

4   Learn

Luke 10:17–24

Working in a rural part of the country, I am currently doing a lot of thinking about the unsustainability of church services, in buildings, led by clergy. I find myself attracted to today's Bible passage as a model of church: we gather together, celebrate what we have seen God doing among us, receive further teaching about how to do it better, and then go out into another week to see what God will do. This dynamic of coming and going, learning and doing, is prevalent in Jesus' discipling of his followers, and the same dynamic has allowed the church still to exist today, a couple of millennia since Jesus walked the earth.

Lifelong learning is a vital part of Christian discipleship. It is when we feel that we have arrived, that we know enough, that we lose the plot. Some people know the joy of lifelong academic learning, going ever more deeply into their chosen area of study, following new trails and ideas. Others learn and grow in their skills: I have recently passed my advanced driving test and am proud of (and, I hope, safer with) my newly gained abilities.

I like the model of apprenticeship for Christian discipleship, because it implies learning at both these levels. We need to understand more as we go on—more of the scriptures, more of the work of the Holy Spirit, more of the world around us to which we are called and sent. But we also need to gain practical skills in order to do the work of Christ more effectively.

A good question to ask ourselves is 'What are we currently learning about Jesus and about following him?' I often meet disciples of Jesus who have the spark of excitement in their eyes, who are enthusiastic about what God is currently doing in them or in their church. Then I meet others whose eyes show deadness, boredom and disillusionment, who can only tell me stories of God at work decades previously. The difference, I believe, between these two kinds of disciples has to do with hunger. When we lose the appetite to learn, we shrivel up as surely as we do if we lose the appetite to eat.

5 Change

Matthew 18:1–5

The material on which these notes are based was first written up as a diocesan discipleship course, and this session was the most controversial of them all. One member of the team told us that if the word 'change' appeared anywhere, her congregation would simply boycott the course. We were reminded of just how deeply scared we often are of this term. (Partly I blame Henry Lyte for equating 'change' and 'decay' in his otherwise lovely hymn!)

Change can mean growth as well as decay, however difficult it can be to convince some people of that fact, and especially when the suggested changes have anything to do with church. Discipleship clearly implies change and transformation, and Jesus makes this explicit in Matthew 18. Unless we change, we can't enter the kingdom (v. 3). He specifically refers to humility in verse 4: transformation can take place only as we adopt the fundamental position of lowliness and eagerness to learn that characterises young children. Paul, in 2 Corinthians 3:18, talks about the change that comes through the work of the Holy Spirit, as we contemplate more and more just who God is.

Another aspect of change is that we become more like Jesus in his holiness. While we can all think of exceptions that prove the rule, young children are generally characterised as innocent and guileless. As they grow, sadly, they learn to sin in all kinds of ways; but Jesus calls us to a childlikeness that is a kind of reverse of that journey, leaving behind all that is wrong and learning to hate sin rather than being excited by it and attracted to it.

It might be difficult to reflect on how we personally have changed along the way of discipleship, but perhaps you can think of someone close to you, and ask yourself what positive changes you have seen in them. Maybe you could even encourage them by telling them what you have seen. One wise pastor used to say to his congregation, 'You're not sinless, but you are sinning less.' That is the kind of change we should all welcome.

6 Go

Matthew 28:16–20

There is an interesting change of language to be seen between the end of Jesus' earthly ministry and the beginnings of the church. In the Gospels, the term 'disciple' is used 268 times, but in the book of Acts the word 'apostle' takes over. Disciples (learners or apprentices) in the Gospels become apostles ('sent ones') after Jesus' ascension. This is the end of the journey that begins, as we have seen, with coming to Christ. Now we are sent by him to repeat the process, to make even more disciples. We are sent to baptise them—that is, to integrate them into Jesus' body, the church—and to make them apprentices in the way of Christ.

Thus the end, the goal, of discipleship is to perpetuate the church. Nowadays we would talk about 'sustainability'—the concern that what we are doing should last beyond the current moment or phase. It is easy to see discipleship in terms of my individual relationship with Jesus, my prayer life, my knowledge of the scriptures, my financial giving and so on. But to see these aspects of life as the goal of discipleship is to miss the point. The goal is to make disciples who can make disciples who can make disciples, and so on, until Jesus returns.

But if the goal of discipleship is to perpetuate the church, the goal of the church is so much more than to perpetuate discipleship. The book of Revelation sets before us a picture of the renewed creation, where mourning and pain will be things of the past, and all that is evil, represented by the sea, will have been removed from the picture entirely (Revelation 21:1–7). The role of the church now is to live and work in that direction, working with the Spirit towards the redemption of all things.

Guidelines

Discipleship remains a hot topic in the church. How have the past few days' readings expanded your thinking about your own discipleship? Where have you felt challenged? Where have you felt encouraged? Have you read anything with which you found yourself in profound disagreement? How have you been inspired to pray for yourself and for the church?

Take a look back at your journey of discipleship so far. What would you say have been the highs and lows for you? When have been the growth spurts, and when the more stagnant periods? Why do you think this is so?

In the next six notes we shall be considering some of the contemporary hindrances to full discipleship. You might like to begin thinking about what aspects you most struggle with, and what you consider to be harmful to the church's calling to make disciples in the 21st century.

If you are part of a church congregation, how does it help you in your growth as a disciple? Do you consider yourself to be well taught and well apprenticed? Are you taking full advantage of activities or groups that are on offer? Whom are you helping in their apprenticeship?

A prayer which you might like to make your own:

Thanks be to you, our Lord Jesus Christ, for your call to discipleship. Most merciful Redeemer, Friend and Brother, as we come to you, follow you, leave the past behind, learn from you, are changed by you and go in your name, may we know you more clearly, love you more dearly and follow you more nearly, for the good of your church and the building of your kingdom. Amen

1 Integrity

Psalm 26

A politician is caught in some act of immorality, probably financial or sexual. His loyal family stand by him, and he defends himself to the waiting media by telling them that his private life is his own business and does not affect his ability to govern, so he has no intention of resigning. We have watched this scene play out many times, and the fact that people swallow it is a mark of a society where integrity seems not to matter any more. Public and private morality have become separated, and seldom does anyone stop to ask the question, 'If you could lie to your wife, how can we trust you not to lie to us, your electorate?'

The Bible has much to say about integrity, and Psalm 26 holds before us an example of true godliness, thus challenging us to it. Yet it is easy for Christian disciples to become infected with the worldview that separates the public from the private. Indeed, one commonly heard accusation of Christian hypocrisy is that people go to church on Sunday to get their sins forgiven so that they can go out from Monday to Saturday and do exactly what they want. This may be far from the truth, but nevertheless we have an image problem!

In verse 2 the psalmist invites God to give him a reality check: do we dare to pray the same prayer? Is our Christian discipleship only superficial or does it run through us like the name through a stick of rock? It is worth noting that, in this psalm, integrity is about the people you do and don't mix with. To be in God's house, in the great congregation, is healthy, as is a life of praise and witness—but to spend time associating with hypocrites and evildoers is seen as profoundly harmful.

The challenge is, of course, about how we can maintain integrity even while mixing with ungodly people. The kind of separation this psalm celebrates is a lifestyle most of us simply cannot manage; nor, I suspect, would we want to, any more than Jesus himself did. How much more important, then, is the company of other Christians to help keep praise alive and integrity valued.

2 Tolerance

In the past, if you wanted to be really nasty to people, you might have called them cowardly or stupid or cruel, but nowadays we have different values, and the greatest insult we can level against someone is to call them 'intolerant'. In schools, churches and other organisations seeking to identify their values, 'tolerance' is always somewhere near the top of the list. So just what is this thing called 'tolerance', and is it a quality appropriate for Christian disciples?

At one level, it's not a bad word. If it means we no longer castigate or persecute people because of their different skin colour, of course we wouldn't want to argue against it. If it means we live in a more diverse society without being cruel to others who are different, I don't have a problem with it. But the fact is that it often means something very different—a refusal to confront evil, a *laissez faire* attitude in which right and wrong no longer matter and everything is relative. And as if that is not bad enough, we have created a lovely postmodern 'tolerant' God—a God of love and certainly not a God of judgement. The language of Romans 1:18 about the 'wrath' of God begins to seem hugely inappropriate.

I can remember the sense of shock and joy, in a recent church service, when we were invited to repent of 'tolerance' during the confession, rather than praying for it in the intercessions. I used to preach regularly that God is not tolerant: he is forgiving, which is a very different thing. God does not tolerate my sin, my weakness in discipleship or my lack of integrity; and nor should I. Rather, he forgives me and works in me by his Holy Spirit towards my perfection. There are times when evil quite rightly makes us angry: just watch the news on TV. There are times when we simply cannot tolerate an action, because it is just plain wrong. Do we believe that God reacts in any way differently? That is exactly why he has revealed his righteousness in Christ.

3 Consumerism

In the developed West, we live in a consumerist society, where we are defined by what we buy and where the motto is so often 'I shop, therefore

I am'. But there is a deeper and more insidious side to consumerism: it is all about broken promises. The advertisers tell us that if we eat their particular brand of cereal, we will have a body just like the girl in the red dress—or that we will get to have breakfast with girls like the one in the red dress. Neither has ever worked for me! And nor have the promises of happiness and contentment made by any of those who wanted to sell their stuff to me. This is because as soon as I get my stuff, there is newer and better stuff on the market—the 'new and improved' version, or the one with cruise control and a bigger engine. Consequently the quest for fulfilment through what we buy will never be satisfied.

As Christian disciples we can still become ensnared by these false promises, and there is plenty of Christian marketing to play the same game. We are offered a better guitar with which to lead worship, the very latest Bible translation, the T-shirt with a new evangelistic slogan on it; you know the kind of thing.

But Christians down the ages have discovered that true fulfilment often comes, paradoxically, through lack of stuff rather than the abundance of it. Jesus' timeless words speak as clearly as ever to those of us who worry about possessions. They may have been aimed originally at those who were worried about food and clothing for survival, but they still speak to today's disciples, anxious about image, respectability and eternal youth. To shout back at the advertising voices coming from our TVs and refuse to join in with their silly games can be a liberating experience, and we can do it confidently because we have a God who already knows what we need. Note also that God knows the difference between what we need and what we simply want, and that, unlike the advertisers, he never breaks his promises.

4 Niceness

Acts 15:35–41

Was Jesus 'nice'? Discuss! In a world of strife and conflict, it is understandable, indeed laudable, that the church wants to model something different and better. We love to be welcoming, we love to get along, and we certainly don't like trouble. After all, wasn't Jesus known for his unconditional love for all? Aren't his disciples meant to be lovely people? Isn't that exactly how people will know that we're Christians?

Yes, but… Tragically it is often the case that you don't have to dig very deeply into the life of a local church before you discover a vipers' nest of nastiness, passive-aggressive behaviour and in-fighting. And 'twas ever thus: not long after making the momentous decision to allow Gentiles to be Christians, two church leaders—Paul and Barnabas—fell out over the issue of pastoral care versus efficiency.

Part of the problem, I believe, is that in our training as Christian disciples, we are seldom taught how to fight well. One of the sessions I used in my parish marriage preparation course was on 'How to have an argument'. Sadly, this subject is seldom on the curriculum of discipleship courses. Of course we will have disagreements, and at times they might get quite harsh, but it is how we handle them that counts. Neither Jesus nor Paul were afraid to confront those with whom they disagreed. Jesus was always taking the Pharisees to task, and, as well as expressing his disagreement with Barnabas, Paul was able to confront those who were in error and to command his younger protégés to do the same. To have left difficult things unsaid, to have simply been 'nice'—or, to return to an earlier theme, 'tolerant'—would have meant that disputes were buried, only to erupt inevitably elsewhere over different issues.

The art of speaking the truth in love, of confronting without destroying, is a delicate one. Jesus' first disciples had plenty of opportunity to see their leaders in confrontation mode, so they learnt to stand for truth and to deal with disputes healthily. God forbid that his church should ever try to be 'nicer' than he is.

5 Laziness

Hebrews 12:4–13

Since the 1980s and the rise of political correctness, the church has really gone off militaristic language. That may be a good thing (although I note that the New Testament isn't so coy about it), but perhaps an important baby has been thrown out with that bathwater—the idea that Christian formation is in some ways like army basic training. The New Testament uses lots of language about hard work, discipline, effort and pain, whereas we can live in a church where we are fundamentally lazy and shirk the effort required to become spiritually fit. We easily hide behind six weeks off chocolate once a year and think that is all that is required to make us into healthy disciples.

Furthermore, in an age characterised by an unwillingness to submit to any authority, we find the idea of being disciplined as difficult as the thought of disciplining ourselves. The suggestion that anyone has the authority to tell us how we should be living our lives, or even that they might point out to us our scope for improvement, is deeply repugnant to us.

This is not a new problem: the Christian church has lived often with the tension between ease and tougher self-discipline. It began with the early monastic movement, in which reform was needed at certain periods to bring monastery practice back in line with its earlier high standards. More recently, the Wesleyan 'Holiness' movement similarly emphasised dedication and discipline as ways to deepen discipleship.

Of course, most of us don't go to quite the lengths of some ancient saints: we tend not to self-flagellate or to live on top of pillars. But could it be that we have gone too far in the other direction? Would a bit more discipline and effort make us better disciples? The author of Hebrews, in chapter 12, encouraged the church to costly, disciplined and painful work; Paul, in 1 Corinthians 9:27, explained how he needed to bring his own body under strict control, just to show it who was boss. It is easy to be ruled by comfort, but far more difficult to make the effort to train ourselves into spiritual health and fitness.

6 Sexuality

1 Corinthians 7:32–38

Sexuality is, of course, a big issue for the church today, but you will be relieved to know that I do not intend to wade into the debate about same-sex relationships, which takes up so much time and attention and causes so many arguments. Rather, I want to go deeper and look at an assumption that drives so much of the debate—the assumption that we all have a divine right to lots of sex. Most people think we're entitled to do it, and to do it with whom and how we like. Whether it is with my fiancé(e), or with that girl or bloke at work we fancy, are secondary issues. The main point is that our society has told us that *not* having sex is wrong, that we're missing out, and that the situation should be remedied as soon as possible so that we can be 'normal'. In other words, waiting is bad and celibacy is downright weird.

However, while the Bible places sexual activity clearly within the limits of marriage, it also recognises, and gives value to, those people who are not involved in sexual relationships at all. Nowhere are they treated as second-class citizens of the kingdom of God. In 1 Corinthians 7, we can see that Paul's highest priority is that people should be devoted to the Lord and ready for his return. If sex becomes a stumbling block, he says, we should do without it; but if doing without it is a stumbling block, then we should get married. This is deeply counter-cultural thinking by our standards, but Paul challenges our priorities radically.

We can also note that the Bible is not anti-sex, as is so often assumed. It just tries to keep sex in its place, and acknowledges that when it comes to this issue, the grass always appears greener on the other side. We only have to look at the number of sex scandals that have rocked, and continue to rock, Christ's church to see what a problem this is, and how much trouble could be avoided were we just to say 'No', and to honour others who have said it.

Guidelines

You may have found this week's readings harsh, sharp, over-confrontational or just plain demanding. You may have experienced discomfort at the politically incorrect nature of some of them. Indeed, the cries continue for the church to accommodate itself more and more to the culture in which we live, to lose its old-fashioned outlooks on various issues and so to become more 'attractive' to the world. History, however, tells us a different story: it is those who have stood firm against the prevailing culture who have changed the world into a better place. The challenge for Christian disciples today is not about how to capitulate in the quest for popularity, but rather how we might stand lovingly for godly values in a world that is heading in the opposite direction.

It is worth listening carefully to your feelings about this past week's readings. Has anything you have read or thought about particularly made your hackles rise? You might like to think about whether you have heard the voice of the Spirit challenging you to a more radical, biblical discipleship. If so, what do you plan to do about it?

A good way to start might be to learn to talk back to the television. Listen to the ideas you are being sold, in the adverts, the news and other programmes, and tell them when you disagree. You will learn to listen more critically, bringing the mind of Christ to bear on the messages with which you are constantly bombarded.

Secondly, revisit the Old Testament, and try to read it while deliberately ignoring the voices of political correctness. What does it really teach us about God, and which of those teachings do not fit with today's culture? Whom will we choose to trust?

FURTHER READING

Graham Cray, *Who's Shaping You?*, Cell UK, 2010.

Roger Walton, *The Reflective Disciple*, Epworth, 2009.

Rick Warren, *The Purpose-Driven Life*, Zondervan, 2002.

Abraham

Have you noticed a growing trend to release prequels to popular film franchises? You might have seen prequels to the Batman, Star Wars or Lord of the Rings series, for example. Prequels are popular with moviegoers because they offer an opportunity to see what happened before the main story. Prequels are popular with film-makers, on the other hand, because they extend the life of a franchise by offering a way forward when a storyline has hit a bit of a dead end.

It might sound like a strange way to start, but the stories of Abraham can helpfully be understood as the Old Testament's prequel. They tell us what happened before God saved his people from slavery in Egypt, giving them Moses, the Torah and the promised land. God's choice of Israel did not come out of the blue, we learn, but was the culmination of his earlier choice of Abraham, his promises to Abraham, and his faithful relationship with Abraham's family.

Prequels are different from introductions, prologues or prefaces, however. Because they are written after the main story has been heard, they often reflect some of the ideas or circumstances of the later time. They also have the capacity to change our perceptions of the main story. Have you ever pulled out the DVD of your favourite movie, for example, to see how different it looks after you've seen its prequel? The Abraham stories are like this. Scholarship suggests that Genesis attained its final form long after the events of the Moses story had been written down, and a developing consensus points to this having happened after Israel's return from exile (that is, in the fifth or even fourth century BC). Abraham's story in its final form reflects the events and concerns of the post-exile community in Jerusalem, struggling under Persian occupation and without the institutions of temple and monarchy that had been so central to Judah's identity before the destruction of Jerusalem by the Babylonians in 587BC.

It also reflects the fears of the community about its continued relationship with its God, Yahweh. What kind of relationship would it be in the future, and how reliable would Yahweh's covenant prove to be? Would the new Israel be any better at keeping Yahweh's commandments and how could they be sure that they would not lose the land again? Israel's story had hit a bit of a dead end: might the old stories of the patriarch Abraham, which had spoken powerfully to the Israelites over many generations, speak now in a new way, offering a way forward?

These short studies are adapted from my book, *Abraham: A journey through Lent*, published by SPCK in 2015.

1 The call

Genesis 12:1–8

Most of us are familiar with the extraordinary account of obedience that opens Abraham's story. When Yahweh chooses Abram, apparently out of the blue, and tells him to leave his country, his kin and his father's house to go to a land that he would be shown, Abram goes. There is no hesitation, no delay, and no discussion of Yahweh's promises of multiplication and blessing in verses 2–3.

Closer reading reveals a slightly more complicated story. If you look back at Genesis 11:31–32, you will see that, in fact, Abram had already set out. He had earlier left his home in Ur of the Chaldeans to go to the land of Canaan with his father Terah, wife Sarai and nephew Lot. Along the way, the family had stopped and settled in the town of Haran, where Terah had died. It is only at this point that Yahweh chooses Abram and calls him to go from his home and travel to Canaan.

Arriving in Canaan, Abram, Sarai and Lot travel through the land, building altars and calling on the name of Yahweh. Recent scholarship points to an earlier version of the story in which Abram did not come to Canaan from outside, but was a local resident. This story opens (perhaps in Genesis 12:5b) with Abram moving through his own land. What is remarkable about the later, additional story of Abraham's journey from Ur is that it resembles the journey taken by the later Israelites who returned from exile in Babylon (like Ur, in Mesopotamia). Like Abram, the returning exiles travelled north to Haran before turning south to Canaan.

This scholarship, together with passages such as Isaiah 51:2 and Ezekiel 33:24, suggests that Abraham was claimed as a foundational father by two different groups. For those Judeans who had not been taken into exile, he was a local who travelled around his own country, while for the returned exiles, Abraham was an immigrant who had made the long and perilous journey from Babylon that they themselves had made. Like Abram, this second group had responded to Yahweh's call to leave Mesopotamia and travel to Canaan. They claimed to be his descendants in a special way and therefore saw themselves as the beneficiaries of Yahweh's promises of increase and blessing (vv. 2–3) and his promise of the land (v. 7).

2 The promise

Genesis 15

If Genesis 12 is often read as a story of Abraham's obedience, Genesis 15 is often read as the definitive story of his faith. For those used to approaching Abraham's story through Paul's account in Romans 4 and Galatians 3, Genesis 15:6 may be understood to encapsulate Abraham's response of faith: 'And he believed Yahweh; and Yahweh reckoned it to him as righteousness.' Approaching this chapter from the point of view of those who have survived the destruction of Jerusalem and the collapse of the temple and the monarchy, however, Genesis 15 can be seen not so much as a story of Abraham's faith as of Yahweh's faithfulness and the reliability of his promises.

At the beginning, the issue for Abram is his lack of a son to inherit his property and to carry on his name. Without one, Yahweh's promises to Abram appear shaky. The story focuses first on Yahweh's promise of many descendants and second on his promise of the land. Without an heir, there seems little prospect for Abram that either will be fulfilled. Abram's questions, 'O Lord God, what will you give me… ?' (v. 2, about descendants) and 'O Lord God, how am I to know… ?' (v. 8, about land), give voice both to Abram's doubt and to the doubt of the returned exiles who were afraid that these promises might prove no more reliable than Yahweh's promises that had already failed, including the promise that there would always be a descendant of David on the throne of Israel.

At each stage, Yahweh takes steps to reassure Abram (and also readers in the fifth century) that he is faithful and his promises are reliable. First, Yahweh takes Abram outdoors and shows him the stars, promising him that his descendants will be just as numerous. Second, through the very strange ritual described in verses 9–17, Yahweh enacts what is essentially a self-curse, taking upon himself all of the responsibility for the future well-being of his relationship with Israel. Yahweh predicts Abram's future in words that comprehend Israel's coming sufferings both in Egypt (400 years, v. 13) and in Babylon (four generations, v. 16), promising that he is in control of history and that although the fulfilment of his promises may be delayed, it will eventually come. Finally, the promises are repeated in a new covenant, in which all of the conditions and all of the responsibility are on Yahweh's side.

3   The visitors

Genesis 18:1–15

In today's story, Abraham offers hospitality to a group of travelling strangers. The identity of his visitors is an issue from the very beginning of the story. Although the reader is told from the outset that Yahweh is visiting Abraham, Abraham sees only three men. What is remarkable about the story is that Abraham treats these strangers as if they are important, running out to meet them, bowing his head down to the ground and preparing a lavish meal.

Over the course of the narrative (scholars have been unable to agree exactly where), Abraham becomes aware of the true identity of his visitor(s), and he and Sarah are rewarded for their hospitality by Yahweh's promise that he will give them a son by Sarah, despite her advanced age. Sarah reacts to this promise in the same way that Abraham reacted to the same promise in the previous story (Genesis 17:17): she laughs, with an uncomfortable laughter, which she goes on to deny. The laughter of Abraham and Sarah (in both cases slightly awkward) relates to the name of the promised son, Isaac, which is built on the root of the Hebrew word 'to laugh'. Further wordgames are played with Isaac's name in later chapters.

In this story, each of the characters plays his or her role according to established principles of hospitality in the ancient world. Without hotels, restaurants and supermarkets, travellers relied on the hospitality of the locals through whose territory they passed, and there were rules and customs to ensure that travellers were housed and fed on their journeys. The system worked both ways, as hosts were able to turn potentially dangerous (hungry and tired) strangers into benign acquaintances. It was typical, too, that a visitor should offer a gift at the end of the visit, although these gifts were usually nominal.

The twist in the story is that Abraham treated ordinary strangers like royalty, not knowing on this occasion (in the words of Hebrews 13:2) that he was entertaining angels. The story implies that Abraham treated all visitors in this way—seeing God in the face of the stranger—but it lets the reader know that, on this occasion, Abraham's visitor was actually God, who rewarded Abraham richly for his righteousness.

4 The 'other'

Genesis 21:1–21

Having been without a son and heir, Abraham suddenly finds himself with two. Here you will see two more instances of the verb 'to laugh'. First, Sarah marvels that God has given her a son at her advanced age (v. 6). The Hebrew is a little ambiguous: Yahweh has literally 'visited' laughter 'upon' her. Is everybody laughing with her or at her? The Hebrew is not clear.

Sarah's feelings are very clear in the second instance, however. She sees Ishmael, the son of her Egyptian maidservant, 'playing' (again the verb 'to laugh') with Isaac (v. 9), and demands that Hagar and Ishmael be cast out so that Ishmael (now about 13 years old) will not inherit in Isaac's place. We read that Abraham was 'very distressed' on account of his son (v. 11). Again the Hebrew is a little ambiguous, but it seems that Abraham's distress is on account of Ishmael, not Isaac. It is striking that this is the strongest statement of Abraham's emotion to be found anywhere in these stories.

God reassures Abraham, promising that he will make a 'great nation' of Ishmael (it would have been remarkable to a fifth-century audience that the son of an Egyptian woman should have received the same promise as Abraham: see Genesis 12:2). Abraham sends Hagar and Ishmael away with only a small amount of bread and water, presumably to die in the wilderness. For a fifth-century BC audience, this story would have played into contemporary debates about intermarriage, resonating strongly with the story of Ezra's demand that the returnees send away their foreign wives and children (Ezra 10:3, 11).

Genesis 21:1–21 does not function as a simple affirmation of Ezra's exclusivist policies, however. Although Abraham sends Hagar and Ishmael away, and God acquiesces, they are not left to die. God seeks out mother and son and provides them with water. He speaks to Hagar directly and makes a promise to her—something that he never does for Sarah. Furthermore, as we have already seen, the promise to make Ishmael a 'great nation' (v. 18) echoes the promise made previously to Abraham (Genesis 12:2), yet God never makes this particular promise to Isaac. Ishmael, the 'other' in the story, might not have been chosen as Isaac is chosen, but nor is he rejected by God or forgotten by Abraham.

5 The choice

Genesis 22:1–19

Having allowed him to send away one son, God now asks Abraham to sacrifice the other. This is one of the most extraordinary, enigmatic and difficult stories in all of the Old Testament. As was the case in Genesis 18:1, the narrator starts by giving the reader important information that is kept from Abraham—the information that God is 'testing' him. We are not told the nature of the test, but later the angel explains to Abraham that his willingness to sacrifice his son shows that he fears God (v. 12).

Scholarly debates about the meaning of the story focus on many of its difficult aspects. Is the story about Abraham's 'obedience' or 'faithfulness'? If 'obedience', was Abraham right to obey such a morally repugnant demand? What does the story tell us about the character of God?

I have given today's reading the title 'The choice' because in it Abraham is required to make a difficult choice—really, an impossible choice—that involves a declaration of allegiance. Is he prepared to give up everything in order to be obedient, or faithful, to God? As 'awe-ful' as we might imagine it was for Abraham to be asked to kill his son, God is asking even more than this from Abraham. All of God's promises to Abraham depended upon his having an heir. Without an heir, the promises were either impossible or pointless. If Isaac were to die, then Abraham's hopes through the divine promises would die also. In order to obey God's demand, Abraham has to renounce all that he potentially has to gain through relationship with God. Is the test, then, rather like Satan's question about Job, 'Does Job fear God for nothing?' (Job 1:9). In other words, will Abraham do God's will even when to do so brings him no personal benefit whatsoever?

One of the many ironies of this story is that because of Abraham's willingness to forgo the promises, God repeats and reiterates them in verses 15–18 (usually thought by scholars to be a later editorial addition). Something new happens as a result of the story, however, which is that the promises, and the relationship between God and Abraham, take on a new shape. Unlike in Genesis 15, where all the responsibility for relationship is on God's side, here Abraham's actions are taken up into and become foundational to that relationship, for the sake of his descendants.

6 The legacy

On its face, Genesis 26 looks like one of the very dullest parts of Genesis. In this compendium of stories, Isaac does a whole series of things that his father Abraham has already done before (twice!), repeating all his father's mistakes (Genesis 12—13; 20—21). He tries to pass off his wife as his sister, and he fights his father's old battles over a confusing succession of wells.

In fact, Genesis 26 is one of the most significant and underappreciated chapters in Genesis. It is here that we get an indication of the legacy of Abraham's actions in chapter 22. The framework of chapter 26 is one in which God extends to Isaac the promises he has previously made to Abraham. If you read 1 Kings 2 and 9, you will see that Genesis 26 (especially verses 3–5 and 24) models God's extension of the Abrahamic promises to Isaac on the extension of the Davidic promises to Solomon, even borrowing some of the language and themes of the monarchic story. The references to Abraham's law-keeping in Genesis 26:5, for example, are entirely anachronistic: in the world of the story, there *is* no law yet.

Verses 3–5 are also highly reminiscent of 22:15–18, and scholars consider these passages to be related, late and additional to their context. Verses 3–5 suggest the significance of Abraham's willingness to sacrifice his son in 22:1–19. Unlike the promises to David, *which failed*, these promises will not fail because they are 'underwritten' by what Abraham did at Moriah. One of the points of the story in which Isaac repeats Abraham's mistakes is to show that God's love and the promises will not leave him: they are guaranteed by Abraham's past actions.

The rest of the chapter illustrates something of what it means to live as God's chosen people among others. Genesis 26 includes the very first narrative in the Old Testament in which conflict between groups of people is peacefully resolved. Yahweh makes room in the land for nations to live together, and, when the nations see that Isaac's family has Yahweh's blessing, they come to him, seeking to participate in it, making sense of Yahweh's promise that the nations of the world would be blessed through the descendants of Abraham.

Guidelines

- Which is likely to inspire the more helpful sermons—Abraham the hero of faith, or Abraham who is a mixed bag of faith, doubt and vulnerability?
- What are today's hospitality codes? What are the implications of your answer for contemporary issues such as immigration?
- What insights does Abraham's story offer for building relationships between people of the three Abrahamic faiths today?
- How does Abraham's story affect the way you read the story of the exodus conquest?
- In what respects does Genesis 22:1–19 prefigure the Gospel accounts of the crucifixion? Does Abraham's story affect the way you read Jesus' story?

God, help us to be like Abraham—to have courage to follow your call, to ask questions and to express our doubts, to laugh in the face of the impossible, to see you in the face of every stranger and, finally, to do your will just because it is. Amen

FURTHER READING:

Joseph Blenkinsopp, *Abraham: The story of a life*, Eerdmans, 2015.

Mark G. Brett, *Genesis: Procreation and the politics of identity*, Routledge, 2000.

Mark G. Brett, *Decolonizing God: The Bible in the tides of empire*, Sheffield Phoenix, 2008.

Diana V. Edelman et al., *Opening the Books of Moses*, Equinox, 2012.

Jon D. Levenson, *The Death and Resurrection of the Beloved Son*, Yale, 1993.

R.W.L. Moberly, *The Bible, Theology and Faith: A study of Abraham and Jesus*, CUP, 2000.

R.W.L. Moberly, *The Theology of the Book of Genesis*, Cambridge University Press, 2012.

Jonathan Sacks, *Not in God's Name: Confronting religious violence*, Hodder and Stoughton, 2015.

Mission in John's Gospel

The Gospel writer himself tells us that his purpose for writing is mission: John's Gospel is 'written that you may believe' (John 20:31). It may be seen as a tract that, in the hands of a skilled practitioner, serves throughout as a missionary document. Mission runs through the Gospel like the name of a seaside town through a stick of rock.

John speaks of Jesus that we might learn of him and from him, in terms of his mission and how we might extrapolate our mission. In places within the Gospel, we get overt calls to mission, but there is much more to mission in the Gospel than these exhortations. In addition to looking for teaching about the responsibility of Christians to engage in mission, we must ask the big questions about the *missio Dei*, the 'mission of God'.

Within the unfolding wonder of John's prelude to his Gospel (1:1–18) we hear this theme expounded: a mission from before time, which is at the very heart of God; a mission in which God has used people, yet primarily a mission that is about his Son, Jesus the Christ. As the renowned missiologist David J. Bosch has said, 'Mission is not primarily an activity of the church, but an attribute of God. God is a missionary God' (*Transforming Mission*, Orbis, 2011, pp. 389–390). However, in recognising the mission in which God has chosen to engage, we must inevitably apply it to the day-to-day realities of our lives. Mission is at the heart of God, and so it needs to be at the centre of who we are.

In its final verses, John's Gospel seems to echo the Old Testament teacher's words, 'Of making many books there is no end' (Ecclesiastes 12:12). The task before us is too great for the constraints imposed upon us by these studies, yet here we can start to ask the questions and begin to apply them to our lives… until he comes!

Quotations are taken from the New International Version of the Bible unless otherwise indicated.

1 Backpacking

John 1:1–14

If ever you go backpacking, the first lesson you learn is to travel light: it is not simply about what you take, but what you are willing to leave behind for the purpose of your trip. Comfort and convenience must be sacrificed! Backpacking requires a certain singlemindedness that isn't everyone's idea of a holiday.

As John begins his Gospel, this truth comes to the fore. The Word may dwell in all eternity, may be the rationale behind all creation, and may share in the very nature of God, yet he comes not only to be with us but to be one of us. By using the word 'flesh' (v. 14), the writer speaks of the brutal reality of our humanness. The Word does not become superhuman, but human like you and me. The very nature of God, the fullness of who God was and is and always will be, dwells within the fullness of what it means to be truly human.

It is this Word, this eternal *logos*, that comes backpacking among us. The term that we translate as 'dwelling' literally means 'tabernacling': as God had dwelt with the people, camping in their midst in the tabernacle in the wilderness, so now Jesus dwells in humanity, backpacking with us through the gospel story. Jesus is the *imago dei*, the 'image of God', revealing to us God's nature, his glory, which is grace and truth. The mission is one of self-revelation, leading to reconciliation; grace and truth can be revealed only when these things are put into action, the inevitable action being reconciliatory. In Jesus we see grace and truth revealed through all that he does, revealed to all humanity in what he does for all humanity.

He travels with us as one of us, exhibiting to us grace and ministering truth, and, as he does so, revealing the image of God, the *imago dei*, to us. Yet we were made in God's image. Our corruption of that image is brought into sharp relief against the untainted image of God. This is true mission—that we might see Jesus and, in seeing him, might catch a glimpse of the wonder, the nature, the very being of God.

2 Beyond ourselves

John the Baptist is walking with his disciples and, on catching sight of Jesus, he points away from himself, beyond himself, to Jesus. Disciples look to their teacher, but this particular teacher wants to point them to a new and greater teacher. Yet there is so much more, for, as John the Baptist identifies Jesus as the 'Lamb of God', he speaks powerfully to those with ears to hear. These words carry the image of the sacrificial lamb, key in atonement theology, and with it Isaiah's image of the suffering servant. Jesus is the one who will be disfigured (Isaiah 52:14), the one in whom others see no beauty or majesty, the despised and rejected one who will be pierced for our transgression and crushed for our iniquities, the very 'Lamb of God' who will be led to slaughter (Isaiah 53:2–7). The one who 'was before' John the Baptist is now here among them; this man whom John baptised the previous day is now the one whom John the Baptist's disciples should follow.

John has caught a glimpse of things beyond himself, beyond this world—a vision of the Spirit of God descending on Jesus at his baptism. John understands what this means: it is the fulfilment of a promise made to him by God, a promise on which he is prepared to stake everything. John, who has gathered followers of his own, gained the adulation of the crowds and caused consternation among the religious leaders, recognises in this fulfilment that it is time to pass the baton to the one for whom he is preparing the way—the Son of God (v. 34, NRSV).

For John, to acknowledge Jesus as the Son of God is to recognise a role that goes beyond his own as a prophet of God. The phrase lacks the ambiguity of 'Son of Man', which might mean a mere mortal or the one who ascends on a cloud to the throne of God in Daniel's vision (Daniel 7:13). John thus brings together the roles of 'Son of God' and 'suffering servant' in a way similar to their juxtaposition in Matthew 16:16–21, where Jesus discusses his identity at Caesarea Philippi and then points toward his suffering in Jerusalem. Jesus was the one whom the Jews were waiting for, and John knew that he had to point beyond himself, for this was his mission.

3 Engagement

We often highlight the fact that Nicodemus came at night, not wanting to be seen, but is that really the point? John shows Nicodemus moving from the darkness of ignorance, later seeking to dampen the Pharisees' blood-lust (7:45–52), to the point where he takes the risk of aligning himself with Jesus at his burial (19:38–42). This journey from darkness into the light of understanding begins with an act of engagement.

Nicodemus comes to Jesus and engages him in discussion. The conversation may seem a strange one to us, but what is occurring here is a discussion between Jewish rabbis—a traditional Jewish theological discussion. The Talmud tells us that rabbinic training was a form of academic engagement where questions were asked of the teacher to draw out the meaning of what was being said. Many of Jesus' statements were not so alien to Nicodemus, yet the questions are asked to draw out more, to take the conversation deeper, so that he might learn from Jesus.

Clearly Nicodemus was a respected Pharisee; after all, he was a member of the Sanhedrin, and so would have been familiar with study and theological engagement. Yet here he humbles himself to take the place of a learner, the place of the questioner, learning from a master.

As Nicodemus engages with him, Jesus opens himself up to Nicodemus. The statements he makes, and the claims he makes for himself, are powerful images that would not have been lost on Nicodemus as a rabbi. Jesus speaks openly in the theological imagery that the Pharisees were familiar with. The image of being reborn is well known within Jewish teaching, the Talmud, where the image of God giving birth to Israel (a repeated metaphor in Isaiah 39 onwards) becomes an idea of individual spiritual awakening. Jesus' engagement is genuine, extensive and risky, given that he is speaking to a member of the ruling council. Yet it is this risk that turns Nicodemus' head and, in the end, will enable him to take a risk for Jesus in helping with his burial.

Real mission requires real engagement and real risk. Mission is never safe if it is to be effective; if people are to believe, they need to know the reality of who we are and who God is.

4 Knowing your place

Standing at the front of a classroom of 15-year-olds is a daunting thing. You can show no fear; they will smell it and grasp on it, and before long you will be at their mercy. Teaching 15-year-olds requires you to be fearless. Yet when another adult is observing your lesson, as so frequently happens these days, you also need a large helping of humility, allowing them to feed back to you how you could have improved your lesson. There is a balance needed between confidence and humility.

John is portrayed as a prophet in the Old Testament tradition—a wild man from the wilderness, an Elijah figure who, having spent time with God, delivered a message demanding that the people turn from their wicked ways. People had been inspired by his message and acknowledged him for who he was. John the Baptist was a someone—an important someone.

John had disciples, people who had given up their way of life to follow his teaching. These followers were not groupies, as I have sometimes heard it said; they were people who had humbled themselves to become learners from their master. So John had importance in the eyes of his society; there were people who followed his every word. Yet John was not self-important. He had that combination of confidence and humility. His sole purpose in life was not about himself or his mission, but about pointing to Jesus.

John knew that this meant stepping back, retreating from the spotlight in order not to detract from Jesus. His disciples were confused, but their master wasn't: everything was about Jesus. Therefore, to serve his own purpose properly, he knew he needed to step back. Too often, we get this wrong. Mission is *our* mission; calling is *my* calling; we make the work of God all about us. 'Where would God be without me to serve him?' Back in the late 1930s, Hoagy Carmichael wrote the song 'I get along without you very well'. Maybe we all need to wake up to the truth that God can cope without us. The mission is to point away from ourselves and point to Jesus.

5 Testifying in weakness

The Samaritan woman had a reputation, though I am pretty sure that she didn't like to think of it. The women of the village shunned her, which is why she was out fetching water at a time when none of the other women would be there, and the men of the village... well, many of them knew her more intimately than simply by reputation. She was used and abused, and everyone knew this.

Yet Jesus had had an impact on her life. He had spoken to her in a public place—something no one else would be seen doing—and had spoken to her knowing the truth of who she was. She was a Samaritan, a member of a grouping that Jews did not associate with. He had asked her for water, yet to have accepted water from her, using her utensils, would have meant opening himself up to her spiritual uncleanness. He had not been seeking to use her, as other men might, but rather had blessed her with his openness and care. Jesus had also spoken openly to her of his true identity, entrusting to her of all people something very precious—that he was the long-awaited Messiah.

She just had to share this news with others; she could not keep it to herself. She knew her place in society—she was there to be used, not publicly acknowledged—and yet now she was making a spectacle of herself to tell the village about Jesus. To do this, she needed to share her weakness: 'Come, see a man who told me everything I've ever done' (v. 29). Yet people listened. They came to Jesus because of her declaration of weakness, and, in hearing for themselves of what Jesus had done and the claims she was making for him, they recognised their own need of a saviour.

Being honest about who we are, acknowledging our own failure and weakness, is an important step in mission. Our culture may cry out for success stories, but this is mainly because we are all too familiar with our own mistakes. We often like to project self-sufficiency rather than a reliance on others. Yet to be truly effective in mission requires us to honest about ourselves and our own unworthiness, and confess our need of Jesus—often a hard lesson to learn.

6 Go on, prove it!

John 6:30–40

John Locke, the father of the empirical tradition in philosophy, has a lot to answer for. Perhaps it's unfair to lay all the blame at his door, but empiricism has led us to a place where the only truth people believe in is forensic truth, truth that can be proved. Many people look to science as the bearer of all answers; for others, the failure of science to provide all the answers, to find the cure for all ills, has led to the view that there is no real truth. Claims and counter-claims are made and the defensive cry goes up: 'Prove it!'

The people demand of Jesus a sign to prove his identity to them. On the other side of the lake, Jesus has fed 5000 people and they have recognised him as the new Moses, feeding the people in the wilderness (see Exodus 16). They wanted to make him king—not because of the wisdom he shared with them but because he had fed them. Yet Jesus withdrew from them rather than receive their adoration (6:1–15).

The adoration is short-lived. He has done it once; now they demand that he do it again. 'What sign then will you give us, that we may see it and believe you?' (v. 30). In other words, 'Prove it!' Jesus answers them by pointing beyond the person of Moses to God (v. 32). It was not Moses who had fed them; it was God. Yet even as he is saying this, surely he is acknowledging that the miracle he has just performed was from God.

As he acknowledges the feeding of the 5000 as an act of God, he then declares that he himself is the very bread of life. This could cause us to ask questions about the eternal meaning of these words, or the connection of this claim to the Eucharist, but let us remain focused on the question of mission. Jesus does not offer proof but rather seeks to take the people's eyes off the act he has done and on to the teaching he has given.

In our proof-based culture, we can be drawn into a similar game. People look for proof as if it identified truth. Yet truth is found in the profound meaning of words. We are called to declare truth, not to seek to prove it.

Guidelines

Scripture is always first and foremost about God and his self-revelation, but the challenge of this focus on mission hits at the heart of our identity.

- Are we journeying with God or have we become settled in our own ways?
- Do we point beyond ourselves to Jesus?
- Do we take risks and give of our very selves when we engage with others?
- Do we have the humility to join in with what God is doing?
- Do we acknowledge our weakness to others?
- Do we tell the story and proclaim God's truth?

As we reflect on John's account of Jesus and what it reveals about mission, none of us can be complacent about our own response. We easily get into ruts; we become our own person, stop taking risks and keep ourselves to ourselves. God's mission quickly becomes 'my' mission, and with ownership comes the desire to do things our own way. We hide behind masks disguising our vulnerabilities and weakness, or perhaps we don't even lift our heads above the parapet.

In the week to come, we will journey on with Jesus to the cross and beyond. It is a dangerous journey to take without some self-awareness. It will be helpful to spend some time in prayerful reflection on our own lives, considering our place in God's mission. This will open up further possibilities for God to speak into our lives through his word.

1 The power of grace

John 8:2–11

Secondary school pupils are an interesting variation on humanity. Classroom behaviour needs to be closely monitored, as the slightest disruption can transform a well-regulated learning opportunity into chaos. When issues occur, I have learnt to hold back the pupils concerned and ask them what they think I should do in light of their behaviour. The surprising reality is that the sanctions they suggest are usually harsher than those I would choose to impose. As a result, my actions are seen as gracious by comparison with their own suggestions, which usually promotes a good relationship and is beneficial for future behaviour.

The story of the woman caught in adultery is full of twists and raises a series of questions about the culture and the circumstances. Why was no man 'caught' with her in adultery? What did she do to get by financially in life? What was her relationship to those who stood in judgement against her? What did Jesus write in the sand? There are so many questions we might ask of the text; more importantly, though, it shouts at the top of its voice, 'GRACE!' This is what we should be talking about.

Grace transforms the situation. Jesus himself, as 'the one who is without sin' (v. 7), could justifiably condemn this woman, and yet he does not. Instead, he offers forgiveness. Grace does not deny the crime or seek to brush it aside; it confronts the issue with forgiveness. Forgiveness is confrontational. Grace is something that we cannot dodge if we are to receive it; yet, even as we receive grace, the power of the truth of the situation changes us.

At the heart of what we believe, in the prayer that Jesus gave us, we declare a conditional clause: 'Forgive us... as we also have forgiven' (Matthew 6:12). Grace is something that must flow through us to others if it is to be effective in our lives.

The power of grace in mission should never be underplayed. Whether people want to defend their actions and attitudes or not, the reality is that the vast majority recognise that they mess up, and the ones who protest their innocence the loudest are often the most aware of their guilt. Confronting such people, in love, with grace and forgiveness, is powerful and transformational. We are bearers of good news, and the best news is always caught up in the power of grace.

2 It is time...

John 12:20–26

The expectant father was snoring happily in his bed, but his wife was not so happy because her contractions had started. She rolled over and shook her husband awake: 'It's time, dear.' He looked at the clock and, in a sleepy haze, said to his wife, 'Time? The alarm isn't due to go off for another three hours...' Then he heard her groan in pain and jumped out of his skin. 'It's time!' he shouted, jumping out of bed. '*It's time!*'

In John's Gospel, after the conversation with his mother at the wedding in Cana (2:4), Jesus seems to spend a fair amount of time pointing out to people that his 'time has not yet come'. Yet when he eventually declares that his time *has* come (v. 23), we are in danger of missing it. This seems such an innocuous little passage, yet, for John, it marks the pivotal moment of Jesus' ministry, for it heralds the time of his coming glorification.

If this is the moment we have all been waiting for, the point to which everything has been building, what is the trigger for it? It appears that the arrival on the scene of 'some Greeks' initiates Jesus' fresh understanding of the circumstances. (Interestingly, there is no record that they ever got to speak to him.)

Who are these inquisitive 'Greeks'? Two feasible answers are offered by scholars: they are either Gentiles or, perhaps more likely, Jews from the diaspora (the dispersion of the Jews to the nations). They are in Jerusalem for Shavout, the Festival of Weeks, the thanksgiving celebration that marks both the wheat harvest and the giving of the Torah on Mount Sinai. What is significant about either group is that they have clearly come from far afield. This is the arrival of the nations at the temple of God—that is, Jesus. They are coming to the mountain of God to worship, as prophesied in the final chapters of Isaiah (Isaiah 60—66).

Jesus clearly recognises the significance of the moment. In mission, recognising the significance of key moments is important. Effective mission requires us to notice the change in the tide, the transformational moment, and seek to address the issues that are arising, rather than simply carry on regardless with whatever we have planned. Jesus is aware of the meaning of the 'signs of the times' and so responds to fulfil his Father's purposes.

3 Mission as Christ-like service

John 13:1–17

There were three of us sitting in the staff room the other evening, heads down, working on our laptops, inputting data from the piles of marking by our sides. The head swept in, but we were all oblivious until he asked, 'Who wants a cuppa?' Before we could speak, he was gathering up our cups and heading in the direction of the kitchenette. It turns out he makes rather a good cup of tea—who'd have guessed?

We are all familiar with the account of Jesus washing the disciples' feet. Jesus, who knew he had all authority and power, disrobed and adopted the role of the lowliest. He washed everyone's feet, even Judas', despite knowing how each person would act towards him. We are aware of all this, and so much more. However, our focus today is on the words of Jesus that follow the events.

Jesus instructs the disciples in mutuality: 'Now that I, your Lord and Teacher, have washed your feet, you also should wash one another's feet' (v. 14). Washing feet was the task of the least important servant in a household. Jesus, in saying this, is challenging them to roll up their sleeves and work alongside each other, not to lord it over others but to serve together in mutuality. If he can humble himself, he the one with all authority and power, then surely they can, can't they?

Insecurity is one of the biggest hindrances to the Christian life. I am not advocating assertiveness training for people in churches—some seem more than capable of asserting their opinions—but a good self-image and a recognition of our identity in Christ are key to healthy churches and healthy mission. It is easy for a preacher to declare that the person who makes the coffee after the service or cleans the toilets during the week is as important in the church as the person standing at the front, but it is not always easy to be the one who, on the week of pulpit duty, rolls up their sleeves and mucks in with others.

This is transformational for church life and transformational for mission; after all, church life should be missional. The minister who serves the soup at lunch club gives a very different impression from that given by the one who sits there and waits to be served.

4 Prayed for and sent

John 17:13–23

The 'high priestly prayer' of Jesus in John 17 contains deep theological truths. It is an overheard yet intimate relational moment between Jesus and his heavenly Father. The whole demands regular meditative reflection, but we shall focus on the issue of mission in this particular passage: 'I pray also for those who will believe in me through [my disciples'] message, that all of them may be one, Father, just as you are in me and I am in you' (vv. 20–21).

This passage highlights one of the simplest and yet most complex truths of mission. It is neither your mission nor mine; it is the mission of the Trinity. We are caught up in the mission of Father, Son and Holy Spirit. This is both simple and profound: the full scope of what we mean by 'Trinity' and what it can mean for us to be caught up in the Trinity is beyond our grasp.

As Jesus prays for unity, or oneness, he is echoing the prayer at the heart of Judaism, the Shema: 'Hear, O Israel: the Lord our God, the Lord is one. Love the Lord your God with all your heart and with all your soul and with all your strength' (Deuteronomy 6:4–5). The opening sentence of the Shema holds two ideas together—the oneness of God and the oneness of the people of God. In Jesus' prayer, too, the two key ideas are combined.

God is at work in the world, working out his mission—a mission that he calls us to be part of. Seeking to identify particular roles for Father, Son or Spirit is a fallacy; God is at work in the persons of the Father, Son and Spirit in all aspects of the mission, moving freely, interchanging, moving together almost like a group of skaters doing an intricate ice dance. As God engages, moves and dances through his mission, we are called to join in—not to make it our own, but to move in step with something that is beyond us.

God invites us, empowers us, enables us and dances with us as we join in. It is God who teaches us the steps, and although God sends us out and, in John 17, even prays for us as he does so, he comes with us and leads the dance.

5 Commissioned to grace

John 20:19–23

Stepping into a new situation—a new house group, church, job or class-room—presents everyone with new opportunities. As a teacher meets a new class, for example, the opportunity of a fresh start is available to all. The only question is whether they will take that opportunity.

As Jesus steps into the locked room in John 20:19, life is transformed. This is the resurrected Lord, and the disciples' whole world has been turned upside down. They are in hiding now, but with this event they will be em-boldened. Nothing can or will be the same.

Jesus greets them with 'Shalom', almost as if this is the most normal thing in the world. Crucified and risen, he reveals the reality to them—that you really cannot keep a good man down! Then he commissions them, transforming them from followers, 'disciples', to those sent out, 'apostles'. But what are they sent out for?

I have heard this passage read many times, but the speaker often stops at verse 22, 'Receive the Holy Spirit', perhaps not wanting to engage with the next sentence. The verse that follows, a verse that may be too quickly dropped, is the key. Yet how are we to understand it? Does God want us to be those who stand in judgement on others?

John's Gospel does not recall Peter's question about how many times we should forgive. Matthew's account of that question (Matthew 18:21–22) echoes and contrasts the account of Lamech in Genesis 4:23–24. Lamech seeks a multiplication of vengeance, while Jesus declares that the same abundance should be applied to forgiveness. Yet here in John's Gospel, Jesus calls upon the disciples to put the idea of multiplying grace into action in the world, to forgive and go on forgiving, that grace may be everything.

We are called and empowered for a mission of grace—not to sit in judgement but to lavish grace on others as God has lavished it on us. Grace is the good news and we, like the first disciples, are sent out to reveal and enact it.

6 Peter loved

John 21:1–19

What does it mean when we say to someone, 'I love you'? The meaning varies depending on the context in which the words are said, yet at its most basic it equates simply to 'I accept you'. Of course, love can mean much more than this, but if there is any sincerity in the utterance, then acceptance is at its heart. Truly to love someone is to accept them, regardless of anything.

Chapter 21 is one of my favourite chapters in John's Gospel. We could discuss its origins, the thrust of the narrative, the lessons it intends to teach and, of course, the knots that verses 23 and 24 tie us into. Similarly, we could delve into the Greek words behind the English translation of the rhetorical interplay between Jesus and Peter. However, in this final reflection of this series, and with our eyes on mission, I want to keep things simple and focus on the five verses from 15 to 19. After all, it is often the simplest lessons that we find hardest to learn.

Jesus loves Peter unconditionally and accepts him unconditionally. Despite all that has gone before and all that lies ahead, Jesus loves Peter. Peter knows that he has messed up many times, and freshest in his mind is the smell of denial that he is struggling to get out of his nostrils (literally, given that Jesus has lit a coal fire on the beach: v. 9; see John 18:18). Yet Jesus' love is unwavering: he both fully knows and fully accepts Peter. This love and acceptance will transform Peter, both in this moment and in the outworking of his life to the point where he willingly gives his life for Jesus.

Mission is mission only when we recognise that we are unconditionally loved, accepted, by God. We cannot be more loved if we succeed, or less loved if we fail; we are already fully loved. We are called to love others, but this is possible only as we recognise the truth that God first loved us (1 John 4:19). And his love is not just for us; it is inclusive of all who will turn to him (John 3:16). As we recognise this unconditional acceptance, as we reflect on it and live it out, we will be transformed by it and through it—transformed for mission. Simple? Maybe, but it is the most important lesson we can learn.

Guidelines

It is impossible to come away from John's Gospel without recognising the responsibility we all have to participate in mission. The Gospel challenges us in many ways:

- Is grace at the heart of who we are? Do we forgive others, recognising how much God has forgiven us? Does grace, both our personal need for it and the necessity of showing it to the world, guide and direct our mission?
- Do we have eyes to see and the desire to grasp the moment to share the truth of the gospel—not shoving it down people's throats but sharing it in such a way as to lift them up?
- As we engage in mission, do we have the humility to wash feet or to fulfil any other act of service to which God may call us? Is mission revealed in both our actions and our words, or does it come across to others as hot air?
- Are we independent agents, doing our own thing *for* God, or are we in step with him? Are we one with the purposes of God, and one with our fellow Christians, working together within the purposes of God?

God is calling us to see grace and to show grace; to work together with each other in humility, and to work hand in hand with God, responding together to his Spirit's leading.

FURTHER READING

Gerald Borchert, *John* (New American Commentary), 2 vols, Broadman & Holman, 1996/2002.

Andreas J. Kostenberger, *The Missions of Jesus and the Disciples According to the Fourth Gospel: With implications for the fourth Gospel's purpose and the mission of the contemporary church*, Eerdmans, 1998.

Tom Stuckey, *Beyond the Box: Mission challenges from John's Gospel*, Methodist Publishing House, 2005.

Derek Tidball, *Meeting the Saviour: The glory of Jesus in the Gospel of John*, BRF, 2007.

Happiness

How do you think of or imagine God? Somewhere, in many of us, is a sense that he is looking for ways to catch us out—that like an overbearing school teacher he loves to find us misbehaving or takes delight in the fact that we have got our fourth declension Latin noun wrong. Yet, the God who made us for himself and in his own image made us to enjoy life in all its fullness. That is what the opening chapters of Genesis portray and that is what Jesus claimed (John 10:10). Those people who turned his loving Father into a mean, spying law-master were abhorrent to him.

Jesus himself portrayed a sense of the vitality of God everywhere he went. Perhaps this is nowhere better depicted than in his love of parties. Jesus wanted to bring out for us the inbuilt happiness potential that he knew God had put within us. Further, both his life and his words show that he was aware of all the kinds of 'happiness' that humans are capable of experiencing, as well as some of the dark paths we can take in the pursuit of happiness, which lead to destruction. His references to 'peace' and 'joy' are markers of this awareness.

So I was delighted when I discovered that Andy Parnham (a medical doctor and committed Christian working with Livability) had developed a course for people to explore the rich texture of human happiness and that, through it, he hoped to open people up very gently to the possibility of a loving, caring God. I have seen the course run with people who are, in some cases, very damaged by life. Interestingly, it has enabled them to ask questions that lead naturally into faith issues.

In these next two weeks of notes, I have, with Andy's support, provided some biblical material to demonstrate that the rich textures of his course are rooted in the biblical witness to the reality of God in Christ. I hope it will encourage us to explore more fully the abundant life Christ came to give us, enabling us to engage with our friends informally when questions of 'well-being' and 'human flourishing' form the topic of conversation. I hope too that many people will want to use this 'happiness' course not only as 'pre-Alpha' material but for its own sake—helping people discover for themselves the happiness that God wants us all to have.

Quotations are taken from the New Revised Standard Version.

The importance of happiness

Revelation 21:15—22:5; Genesis 1:20—2:3

One of the ways we can discern the purposes of God for humankind is through the Bible's depiction of the 'end times', which often sounds a powerful note of celebration. Festivals, weddings, pilgrimages and feasts are all social events that are intended to celebrate and promote human happiness, both deeply personal and corporately expressed.

Today's passage from Revelation brings a similar sense that God's intention for humankind is profound happiness. Indeed, the earlier verses of chapter 21 pick up the celebratory metaphor: the 'new Jerusalem' is 'prepared as a bride adorned for her husband' (21:2). Hence the city is bedecked with amazing jewels and shimmers with radiance: 'The wall is built of jasper, while the city is pure gold, clear as glass' (v. 18). The foundations are adorned with all kinds of richly coloured jewels. It has, like the ideal bride, perfect proportions.

But the sense of happiness is broader than this. To start with, all that is detrimental to or a perversion of human happiness is banished from this place (see 21:8, 27; 22:3). Nothing accursed will be there. It is completely safeguarded. Then its tranquillity and aesthetics are guaranteed by the river that flows through its central street. So also is its fertility, as there is 'the tree of life' on either side of the river (22:1–2).

This resonates with Genesis 1—2, which is equally full of the sense of happiness that God intends for us, with the abundance and variety of plant and animal life and their guaranteed fruitfulness. The very nature of humankind as God's image and the blessing endowed on us point towards the Creator's desire that the world should be the home of happiness.

In Revelation we can note two further indicators of the happiness quotient. First, the tree of life is always fruitful and is 'for the healing of the nations' (22:2). God's original intention is now fulfilled. Second, the new Jerusalem contains 'the glory and the honour of the nations' (21:26). All that is beneficial and enriching from the culture and achievements of all people will be accessible.

The climax, the pinnacle of human happiness, is that God is fully worshipped and people will 'see his face' (22:4). Here we are given insight into God's deep desire for and commitment to human happiness in all its dimensions, physical, relational and spiritual.

2 The 'joyous' God

Psalm 65

I cannot think of a more potent image of happiness than this: 'You make the gateways of the morning and the evening shout for joy' (v. 8). The totality of day and night is iridescent with happiness. It is as though, whenever we look out on life, our eyes are drawn to these magnificent gateways and they scream at us beauty, delight, enjoyment and satisfaction. They stand as sentinels that border the parkland in which we are situated; they are decorative in themselves and the views through them are even more breathtaking—and God is the cause of all this.

No wonder the psalmist says, 'Happy are those whom you choose and bring near to live in your courts. We shall be satisfied with the goodness of your house, your holy temple' (v. 4). The impression given by these verses is that God has selected us to be his favourites, to live near him, to have open access to him. All the provisions he has are made available to us. There is nothing we could desire that will be withheld from us. As we saw in Revelation 22:3–4, the key feature of human happiness is being able to see God 'face to face', so to speak.

God offers us forgiveness for our sins and complete release from the baggage we would otherwise have to carry that could spoil our sense of enjoyment (v. 3). He controls all the alien forces that might actually threaten our security (vv. 6–7), and he has already delivered his people from their enemies (v. 5).

The climax of this picture of the joyful and joy-making God is his work in creation: 'You crown the year with your bounty; your wagon tracks overflow with richness' (v. 11). The whole description of fruitfulness and harvest (vv. 9–13) is almost too much to bear. All the prosperity, all the joyfulness of creation is experienced as the outworking of God's life flowing into the world (compare Revelation 22:2).

The world at its most fruitful, colourful, productive and lively is a reflection of the nature of God. So it follows that when we are vibrating with happiness, we are actually reflecting his nature: we are made in his image.

3 The blessing of God

This passage claims that the key to happiness is in keeping the ways of wisdom (v. 32). It goes on, 'Happy is the one who listens to me, watching daily at my gates, waiting beside my doors' (v. 34).

To understand this as some kind of imposition—as an obligation and duty to follow a set of rules that claim divine authorisation and are therefore external and oppressive—is as far wide of the mark as is possible to go. These verses are actually claiming that in his generosity God has made human beings with a natural propensity to do what is right and therefore to enjoy happiness. We can perceive this more clearly if we note three points from the passage.

Wisdom is embedded in creation. Its reality is woven into the very structures of existence. Verses 22–31 express this idea in various ways. Wisdom precedes creation: it is the essence of all that exists (like 'the Word' in John 1). Wisdom is built into the fabric of all reality. The very way the universe is constructed is through 'wisdom'. When the physical world is operating properly, it is echoing this inbuilt wisdom

However, human society and culture are also infused with wisdom (vv. 12–20). Those who rule, when they rule well, are utilising the divine resource of wisdom inherent in all societies. Not only Israel's kings but all kings can have access to it. When justice is being properly administered and is effective in maintaining a happy society, it is because wisdom is being exercised.

In addition, wisdom is the source of delight, joy and happiness: 'I was the master worker at his side. I was filled with delight day after day, rejoicing always in his presence, rejoicing in his whole world and delighting in the human race' (vv. 30–31, NIV). This wisdom is clearly not associated with boring routine; its essence is delight, rejoicing and happiness.

It is unsurprising, then, that those who live out the inherent qualities of the universe are successful and happy (vv. 15–21). Wisdom is God's happiness principle and is available to all who will seek it and apply it in their lives.

4 The overflowing land

Deuteronomy 6:3–5; Psalm 104:10–19

One of the three key ways in which humans experience or achieve 'happiness' is through pleasure. Pleasurable sensations are an important contributory factor in our sense of well-being. Of course, if we are depressed, their impact is suppressed, and if they are illicit pleasurable sensations, then their contribution to our sense of well-being can be reduced. However, in normal circumstances, pleasurable sensations make us happier. God knows that and makes provision for us.

Today's Bible passages reflect his provision. 'A land flowing with milk and honey' (Deuteronomy 6:3) indicates that both our basic nutrients and the pleasure of unlimited sweetness are promised by God, who recognises that humans have legitimate sensory needs beyond mere survival. This description of the land that God gives to his people occurs frequently.

The language of Psalm 104 is even more effervescent: God gives 'oil to make the face shine, and bread to strengthen the human heart' (v. 15). 'Bread' here, in Hebrew, means all foods—doughnuts, chocolate biscuits, you name it and it can be included. Pleasure indeed! In addition, the equivalent to our perfumes and skin treatments is involved in this generosity of God, for 'oil' is not primarily for cooking but to bring a sense of significance, ease and affluence.

The abundance is not restricted to resources for humans; the psalm describes a general sense of pleasure throughout creation—for birds and goats and lions (vv. 17–18, 21). As the superfluity of nature programmes on TV shows us, from gardening to Patagonian wilderness, human happiness is not restricted to our personal individual experience of pleasures but can be enhanced by glimpsing the sensory pleasure of other people and other creatures.

However, for the readers (or reciters) of these scriptures, all these sensory pleasures are extended, deepened and sustained by an underlying worldview that recognises God as their provider. The psalm also shows that God orders his world so that his provision may be sustained. It emphasises repeatedly, 'You make… you cause… you set…' This reduces our anxiety that such pleasures may be withdrawn suddenly and capriciously. Beyond the immediate sensations is the sense that this is an orderly world and that God takes delight in our delight, thus adding to our happiness.

5 The overflowing wine

John 2:1–12; Psalm 4:6–8

Pleasurable sensations may be enhanced by the context in which they occur (or, indeed, diminished by the context if it conflicts with the pleasure—think of a wedding banquet where there is a row between family members).

As we read John 2, we find ourselves in an exhilarating context—a wedding feast. It is a time for relaxation, social interaction, excitement and satisfaction in the knowledge that the nurture of children has resulted in a marriage, with all the human fulfilment that it entails. There is colour in the clothes and perfume in the air, as well as lively music and dancing all around. This day (or week!) is the culmination of months of planning and promises good things to come, as a new family, probably with children to follow, is being launched. A rich cocktail of activity and emotions underlines the pleasure to be had in social drinking.

But there is a serious problem! The wine has run out (v. 3). So the pleasure and the happiness associated with it are actually dependent on a sensory experience, and the context cannot compensate. In the end, of course, Jesus turns 150 gallons of water into wine—an overflowing amount, to ensure that the happiness of the guests is not spoilt. It is not only a more-than-generous quantity; the wine is also of superb quality.

However, buried within this story are some indications of factors that limit the happiness we gain through pleasurable sensations. Andy Parnham writes: 'There are two key problems with pleasure as a source of happiness: first, pleasure fades. Second, pleasure habituates… the more you experience a pleasure, the less happiness you receive from it' (Happiness course, Session 2, 'Is pleasure enough?'). In addition, drinking (too much) wine itself dulls the awareness of the pleasure. This is why the best wine is normally served first (v. 10); later on, people won't notice the deteriorating quality.

There is validity in experiencing happiness from pleasurable sensations. Psalm 4 recognises this, while also indicating that such sources of happiness are not ultimate, and can be surpassed by our relationship with God: 'You have put gladness in my heart more than when their grain and wine abound' (Psalm 4:7).

6 The overflowing heart

Song of Songs 2; John 7:37–39

Song of Songs can probably claim to be the most sensory book in the Bible: 'Let him kiss me with the kisses of his mouth! For your love is better than wine, your anointing oils are fragrant, your name is perfume poured out; therefore the maidens love you' (1:2–3).

These verses are full of sensory images of touch, taste and smell. Throughout the book, visual and audible images are also plundered in the attempt to capture something of the pleasure of sensual love, as chapter 2 indicates well. From lilies and apple trees to gazelles on mountaintops and bursts of flower after rain, to turtle doves cooing and the fragrance of the vine in blossom—it's all there. The climactic image is this: 'With great delight I sat in his shadow, and his fruit was sweet to my taste. He brought me to the banqueting house, and his intention towards me was love' (vv. 3–4).

These metaphorical images, along with the implied sexual ones, make it abundantly clear that God has constructed a world in which the responses of all our senses to its varied and intense beauty can contribute to our overflowing happiness.

But there is more to this rainbow of happiness than some kind of mechanical response register: human happiness is far more complex than that. Verses 8–9 ('Look, he comes… Look, there he stands') indicate that anticipation can increase happiness (unless, of course, the happiness is frustrated). A sense of security also enhances the experience: if we fear that it might suddenly come to an end, our capacity to enjoy the pleasure of the moment is seriously threatened (see v. 15). Further, the book implies that there is a communal dimension to happiness, as indicated by the references to 'daughters of Jerusalem' (v. 5 and elsewhere).

The festival mentioned in John 7:37 was itself a very sensory experience, a kind of *son et lumière*. Jesus, we note, uses another sensory image to indicate the gift that he offers—the deep happiness of quenching thirst with pure cool water (compare Isaiah 55:1–3). But such sensory images find an even greater fulfilment for us as humans in our relationship with God. This is the claim that Jesus makes: he is able to cause rivers of living water to flow out of us.

Guidelines

Is it selfish to desire to be happier or to seek for greater happiness? Reflect on the scriptures we have read this week, and the following paragraph:

Happiness offers myriad rewards—not just for the happy person, but for his or her family, workplace, community, nation and society. Working on how to become happier, the research suggests, will not only make a person feel better but will also boost his or her energy, creativity and immune system, foster better relationships, fuel higher productivity at work and even lead to a longer life.

Sonja Lyubomirsky, *The How of Happiness*, p. 2

Do you agree? If so, why do you think it is likely to be the case? Could it be that this is connected to the way God has made us to function?

1 Family relationships

Genesis 45:1–15

Genesis 45 is a deeply moving account of Joseph's restoration to his family. Years earlier, his brothers resented him. They thought of murdering him but, in the end, sent him captive as a slave to Egypt. This led to all kinds of cruelty and degradation in Joseph's experience for many years—including slavery and imprisonment on a false charge of rape. Eventually he became second-in-command to Pharaoh, with the responsibility for supervising food storage and distribution during seven years of famine.

When his brothers, desperate for food, come to Egypt and encounter their brother without recognising him, Joseph, after many ploys, reveals his identity to them. He has every reason to torture and kill them—and that is what they must have expected. Yet we read, 'And he kissed all his brothers and wept upon them; and after that his brothers talked with him' (v. 15).

By now, Joseph has every kind of human pleasure available to him—wine, women and song included. He is extremely successful and honoured in Egypt beyond measure. He is powerful and secure. But what he longs for so deeply is to be restored to his family, not only his brothers but his father as well (vv. 9–11).

Here we have a remarkable illustration of the importance of relationships, especially positive, supportive, sustainable relations with family members. As Andrew Parnham writes in his 'Happiness' course, 'The yearning to attach and connect, to love and be loved, is the fiercest longing of the soul. Our need for community with people is to the human spirit what food and air and water are to the human body' (Session 3, 'Listen', Part 2).

But this passage illustrates even more. Andrew goes on to explain how we are all vulnerable because of our past experiences. In our heart, pain can turn into resentment, which not only destroys our felt experience of happiness but also corrupts us. The antidote is not revenge (as we naturally think) but forgiveness. Joseph had ample opportunity to exact revenge, yet he totally forgave his brothers for the many years of suffering. That forgiveness included release from their guilt, acceptance into his embrace and emotional reassurance, and it went on to encompass provision for their well-being. Joseph knew that happiness inevitably involves family relationships and their restoration.

2 Friends

Philippians 4:10–23

The TV programme *Friends* is one of America's most successful exports to the United Kingdom. It explores the joys and sorrows, the depths and superficialities of friendship in today's world. In our society, where there is often considerable alienation within families (or separation, which results in less experience of the innate happiness that derives from good family life), friends become an ever more important component of our relational happiness.

Today's reading provides a window into the heart of Paul as it shows us the importance of his friendships with people in the church at Philippi, which he had founded. Right from the start of his experience there, the offer of friendship by Lydia was an important component (Acts 16:11–15). As he writes to the Philippians, he recalls the pleasure that he had from their generosity to him, and it seems that the memory of it rekindles that happiness (vv. 15–16). He also indicates that their renewed expression of concern and friendship has brought him deep happiness (v. 10).

Here we see that the happiness brought by friendship involves a sense of being valued, remembered and helped. It is increased, too, by the practical experience of these factors. Paul amplifies the sensory nature even of relational pleasure when he describes it as a 'fragrant offering' (v. 18). The first use of this term in the Old Testament is in Genesis 8:20–21: 'Then Noah built an altar to the Lord… and offered burnt-offerings on the altar. And when the Lord smelt the pleasing odour, the Lord said in his heart, "I will never again curse the ground… nor will I ever again destroy every living creature."'

The context of these verses is the end of the flood. When Paul uses the same image of sacrifice, it indicates how profound friendship may be. So powerful was the experience of pleasure and happiness felt by God during Noah's offering that it caused him to decide to undo part of the curse that followed Adam and Eve's disobedience (see Genesis 3:17).

Twice Paul uses the idea of being 'fully satisfied' (vv. 18–19) to indicate the settled happiness that the awareness and experience of good friendship brings to people. Friends in our lives can be a profound source of lasting happiness.

3 Friendship with God

2 Corinthians 5:16–21; Luke 19:1–10

The closer people are to us, both physically and emotionally, the more potential they have for affecting the level and awareness of happiness in our lives. This is true positively and negatively. The negative impact is experienced most acutely through betrayal or bereavement.

For some of us, the genetic connection is overwhelmingly powerful, as was the case for Joseph. We do well, however, to remember that 'family' is not straightforwardly a matter of genetics. Our experience of family is mediated by the social context, involving security and provision, multi-level interactions, work as well as play, significance (we have a valued place in a hierarchy) and so on. For others, friends play a dominant role in the relational component of happiness (or, indeed, misery). However, 2 Corinthians 5 makes it clear that we are capable of positive, happiness-generating relationships not only with family and friends but also with God.

Divine friendship, Paul tells us, is mediated through Jesus Christ. One of the best-known and most potent biblical examples is Jesus' encounter with Zacchaeus the tax collector. Zacchaeus is perceived to be a loner: he had to climb a sycamore fig tree to see Jesus because he was too short to see over the crowds, so presumably he had no family or friends who were prepared to make room for him.

Yet Zacchaeus' relationship with Jesus becomes so significant that he is prepared to jettison his wealth in order to put his life in good order. All the power and prestige that money could gain for him (and the happiness that, we might assume, would go with them) are worth nothing compared with the happiness of his friendship with Jesus and his restoration of happiness to the poor and to others whom he may have defrauded. Salvation has come 'to this house,' says Jesus (v. 9), for he has been restored to his rightful place in the family of God.

In this story we see enacted the process of reconciliation to which Paul refers in 2 Corinthians 5:18–20. The ultimate source of our happiness is in a renewed relationship with God, and this is true not only for us but for God himself. There is 'joy in heaven' when our friendship with God is restored (Luke 15:7, 10).

4 The need for meaning

Ecclesiastes 12:1–8

'Vanity of vanities, says the Teacher; all is vanity' (v. 8). This is not a very cheerful start to a note on biblical insights into happiness—and the preceding verses may not seem much better. They give a brilliant description of the limitations that come with older years. The recognition of a decrease in physical pleasures and a decline in faculties such as sight and hearing is mixed with a gloomy sense that the way the older person perceives the world is also the way the world actually is. Personal physical limitations take on a universalised significance in the psyche. Songs cease, fears increase and even the beauty of the flowering almond tree fails to stimulate a sense of *joie de vivre*: 'desire fails'. And at the end of it, 'All must go to their eternal home, and the mourners will go about the streets' (v. 5).

However, the point of all this is provided in the opening verses. This passage is acknowledging that, given the long-term view and experience of human life depicted here, our life on its own cannot provide the meaning and purpose that are intrinsic to a full life of happiness. So, then, 'remember your creator in the days of your youth' (v. 1).

Andy Parnham reports Prince Charles as saying, 'There remains deep in the soul (if I dare use that word) a persistent and unconscious anxiety that something is missing, some ingredient that makes life worth living' (Session 4, p. 14). Even if we focus on what motivates us—whether adventure, fame or service—and even if we select actions that maximise these internal forces to develop a sense of meaning, fulfilment and happiness, will they be enough in the end? According to the Teacher in Ecclesiastes: no. Only if we have lived our lives in conscious awareness of and partnership with our Creator is there the possibility of an enduring happiness, even as life fails us.

The reason for this, I suggest, is as follows. It is only if we have trained ourselves to see life (including our individual life) as God's gift and to perceive it from the perspective of his purposes that we will be able to surmount the temptation to let our increasing restrictions dominate our assessment of how the world really is.

5 The source of meaning

Hebrews 12:1–13

For humans, there are potentially two ways to gain a sense of meaning and, through that, of enduring fulfilment and happiness. 'Intrinsic' meaning is meaning that we generate from within ourselves, by, for instance, considering ourselves important, successful or kind. However, we often seek to bolster intrinsic meaning by gathering around us items or people that give us corresponding feedback. For example, we may frame a degree certificate and put it on the wall, or associate mainly with people who tell us how wonderful we are. As these illustrations show, it is extremely difficult to sustain intrinsic meaning totally from within.

'Extrinsic' meaning is meaning that other people, objects or situations provide for us. The weakness in gaining our meaning from beyond ourselves is that it leaves us vulnerable. The providers of our sense of meaning can withdraw their gift, or, if it comes through an object or status, it can be destroyed. It may even lose its importance for us through a tragedy such as bereavement: if our meaning is provided by the love of our partner, what happens if that person leaves us for another? Devastation! It is also clear, therefore, that extrinsic meaning cannot exist for us without being internalised and becoming intrinsic.

The writer to the Hebrews explains that Jesus gained meaning (and, ultimately, joy) by fulfilling God's plan for him, even though it involved death on the cross. His significance came from knowing who he was, from accepting the purpose of God for his life willingly, and from a future hope.

Here are three clues for making our significance (and therefore our happiness) secure. First, Jesus' sense of 'who he was' was not found in physical prowess or even miraculous powers. It was given to him by God: he was God's Son. Nothing could change this relational reality, although his perception of it could change (see Matthew 27:46). We too can be children of God.

Second, Jesus always sought to fulfil the purposes of God—and so can we. Although, unlike Jesus, we shall sometimes fail to internalise God's purposes totally and will stray from them, through repentance we can get back on track. Finally, we can share the same future hope for the coming of God's kingdom, knowing that it depends ultimately on God, not ourselves. Happiness as a sense of meaning is most completely experienced and sustained through God.

6 The power of meaning

Proverbs 8:14–36

We return for a second look at Proverbs 8, and we begin by noting a detail. In the NRSV, the word translated 'happy' (vv. 32, 34) is rendered as 'blessed' in Matthew 5:3–11, whereas the NIV uses 'blessed' for both passages. The point to note is not the scholarly justification for either preference but the semantic connection between biblical 'blessedness' and 'happiness'.

More importantly, we need to appreciate who is making this claim ('Happy are those who keep *my* ways... the one who listens to *me*') and to recognise its importance. This passage plays on the appeal of the adulteress or the prostitute, who claims that entering her door is the way to happiness (see Proverbs 9:13–17). Proverbs often challenges this claim (see, too, 7:6–23). Times don't change that much! But here 'wisdom' presents herself as the source of true happiness, in opposition to the powerful but ultimately false offer of happiness through sexuality.

Proverbial wisdom can be expressed in fairly trite sayings, such as 'A gossip goes about telling secrets... To guarantee loans for a stranger brings trouble... Like a gold ring in a pig's snout is a beautiful woman without good sense' (11:13, 15, 22), but it is far more than that. Wisdom is hidden from both the heavens and the depths, yet God understands it (Job 28:23–24). Wisdom in Proverbs 8 is the core of the universe, the sense of and expression of the deep mystery and meaning intertwined with the whole of reality.

Everyday wisdom, if followed, is meant to provide us with a 'happy life'—one marked by physical pleasures and good relationships. But this more profound, embedded wisdom indicates that true happiness can only be found by engaging with God: 'For the Lord gives wisdom' (2:6).

In the New Testament, Wisdom is identified with Jesus (Colossians 1:15–20). There it is revealed that this core, the hidden reality within the universe, is love—God's kind of love. Hence, if ultimate happiness is to be found only through engaging with meaning, then ultimate meaning is to be found only through responding to and living out God's love. As 1 John 5:12 puts it starkly, 'Whoever has the Son has life; whoever does not have the Son of God does not have life.' By life 'here' is meant eternal life—the life of true happiness.

Guidelines

- Are there people in your life from whom you have been parted, whether by bereavement, serious illness or life circumstances, whose absence damages your sense of happiness? What can you do about this?
- Are there people who have seriously hurt you, so that you are cut off from them by a destructive barrier? What can you do in terms of offering forgiveness and seeking reconciliation with them? What might hinder you from taking these steps?
- Are there people you have hurt, or who feel (even wrongly) that you have let them down? What can you do about these situations?
- If Prince Charles is right that people have a sense of 'something missing' from their lives, how can we use this common yearning for happiness as a pathway to help them discover that they are looking for God? Do you know people you can pray for, whom you can help along on this journey?
- Give thanks to God for all the things, experiences and people that contribute to your happiness and well-being. Pray for those who are less well provided for than yourself.

FURTHER READING

www.livability.org.uk/blog-and-resources/training-and-events/
   the-happiness-course

S. Lyubomirsky, *The How of Happiness*, Piatkus, 2010.

M.E.P. Seligman, *Authentic Happiness*, Nicholas Brealey, 2003.

Song of Songs

At the heart of our Bible lies a small, mysterious gem: 'The Song of Songs, which is Solomon's' (1:1). It expresses, in seductively beautiful lyric poetry, a passionate sexual relationship between a man and a woman.

Written almost entirely in direct speech, the book is not a narrative with a plot (although this has not prevented some readers trying to find one, usually involving either two or three main characters). The lovers, who are not identified, simply speak to each other and about each other. This creates a sense of immediacy: the relationship is not described from outside, in the past tense, but is taking place in front of our eyes, as we overhear and observe. However, the subtle poetry abounds in ambiguity: are the lovers speaking of past experiences or present delights, or are they dreaming and fantasising about the future—or all of these mixed together?

From very early times, Jewish and subsequently Christian interpreters have seen a divine–human relationship in the Song. Allegory transforms the lovers into God and those who seek or belong to God. More recent scholars, however, have rejected this approach, rightly reclaiming the Song as erotic love poetry. Human sexuality and physical intimacy are explored, expressed and celebrated here as good, as they are in the opening chapters of the Bible. But the intriguing question still lingers: in addition to expressing human sexual love and desire, can this beguiling text express our longing for intimate connection with God?

The opening verse of the Song mentions Solomon. This could indicate that Solomon is the author or that the book was later connected with him as a traditional source of wisdom and archetypal lover, having been written by someone else. No further clues are given about the author's identity.

This poem (or collection of poems) declares itself to be a song—indeed, the ultimate, the finest of songs, as indicated by the repetition in its title (compare the phrases 'king of kings' and 'holy of holies' elsewhere in scripture). It has inspired songwriters down the centuries, and in these notes we shall draw on some of the most recent musical evocations of the biblical Song, to see how they may enrich our encounter with it. (All the works cited can be heard through online streaming services.)

Biblical quotations are taken from the New Revised Standard Version.

1 Mutual delight

Song of Songs 1:2—2:7

'Here's a woman singing.' Kate Bush's 'Song of Solomon' highlights the predominant voice of the woman in the biblical book, taking the initiative and expressing her sexual desire for the man. The female voice is also emphasised in Patrick Hawes' 2009 classical version of the Song, through the lead constantly given by the soprano soloist.

Female voices speak most of the words in the biblical Song (this is not always evident in our translations, but is clear in the original). This is the only book in the Bible in which a woman's thoughts and words are so clearly predominant; we experience the relationship from her point of view. This intriguing fact has prompted speculation about the author. Was it written by a man, perhaps imagining his ideal woman who desires him strongly, or could it have been written by a woman? Some scholars support the latter view, arguing that the Song conveys feminine perspectives with particular subtlety and awareness.

In an attempt to clarify who is speaking, some translations helpfully indicate 'she' and 'he' in the margins. Others unhelpfully distinguish between the 'lover' (man) and 'beloved' (woman)—titles which may suggest that the man is active in the relationship, while the woman remains passive. In the Song, both the man and the woman are active in speaking, seeking each other and initiating loving intimacy, right from her passionate opening exclamation, 'Let him kiss me...!' Mutuality is evident: each of the lovers gives protection and nourishing delight to the other (1:13; 2:3).

These lovers find themselves (literally or in their imaginations?) in a sensuous garden of delight. Love stimulates their senses: the scent of costly perfumes may waft in the reader's imagination, along with sights and smells of blossom, grass, cedar, cypress, flowers and fruit (1:12–14, 16–17; 2:3). The natural world in which the lovers live is not ignored or displaced, but is affirmed in their love-talk. Romance transforms the natural world: colours seem brighter, tastes are sweeter and everything is more intense —life's joys and, as we shall see, also its agonies. For lovers, the season is spring. Some scholars suggest allusions here to the opening chapters of Genesis: paradise is regained in the exotic garden of lovemaking.

2 Springtime and searching

Song of Songs 2:8—3:5

The woman has spoken of 'love… better than wine' and being 'faint with love' (1:2; 2:5). Sinéad O'Connor captures something of this inebriated 'swooning' experience in her gently breathless version of the Song, 'Dark I am, yet lovely'. Its elegant waltz tempo reflects the rhythmic dance of mutuality in the relationship between the lovers, although only the woman's voice is heard in O'Connor's solo; in the biblical Song, man and woman's voices alternate.

The woman depicts her lover approaching from a distance, bounding across the countryside, seemingly oblivious to all obstacles, until he arrives at the house where she is and can peer inside. She senses him close at hand, enticing her to come out from behind her protective walls. He woos her with a vivid evocation of the delights of spring, which they can experience together if only she will come out and join him.

The woman responds with a cryptic warning about 'little foxes that ruin vineyards' (2:15), perhaps a metaphor for other young men who may find her attractive. Is this playful teasing, warning her lover not to take her for granted? Teasing can help puncture self-importance and restore fun to a romance—or it can wear down fragile self-esteem if carried too far. But she also declares, 'My beloved is mine and I am his' (v. 16). Later she will mirror this expression with 'I am my beloved's and my beloved is mine' (6:3). They belong to each other, with no sign of power struggles between the partners or a desire by either one to dominate the other.

From the delights of spring, the Song moves suddenly into a crisis for the couple. In the kind of fantasy or dream-like moments that recur at night, her love seems to be missing; her yearning for him leads her out to search the darkened streets. Eventually her lover is found, grasped and brought into a secure and intimate place. These agonised verses are also heard in Sinéad O'Connor's version of the Song, which is unusual in highlighting the woman's search for her absent lover and her fears of loneliness: 'Tell him don't leave me alone' is her closing line. Security and anxiety interweave in O'Connor's song, as they do in the biblical Song, and in the experience of many couples.

3 A royal wedding

Song of Songs 3:6—5:1

Are these lovers married, or getting married? The Song has often been read at weddings, and some scholars suggest that this was part of its original design. A wedding is mentioned in 3:11, and the woman is repeatedly described as a bride (4:8–12; 5:1). We see a magnificent royal procession; it is unclear whether the couple are truly Solomon and his bride or simply imagining themselves as king and queen for their special day.

Now for the first time the man describes the woman (4:1–8). His description of her features seems opaque and puzzling to us, concealing as much as revealing. Yet the intriguing metaphors used in these and later descriptions prevent the passages from becoming voyeuristic and pornographic: in the couple's depictions of each other we see naked bodies clothed in metaphor, as Cheryl Exum puts it. Similarly, 5:1 (the central verse of the whole book) suggests sexual consummation in its evocative imagery of feasting. The poet uses language that is somehow both erotic and reticent at the same time.

Some readers find echoes here of other biblical books—for example, in the image of 'a column of smoke' moving up 'from the wilderness' (3:6) and the descriptions of an ornate procession. Does all this suggest the people of God in Exodus, with the ark of the covenant being carried and the elaborate furnishings of the tabernacle and temple (3:10)? Is the woman being equated to 'a land flowing with milk and honey' (4:11; see Numbers 13:27)? If so, the Song might suggest God seeking intimate relationship with God's people, the bride.

These allusions, if present, are at best faint hints, not prominent in the text. It is human love that is being celebrated in the images of a fertile and nourishing garden of delight. A reciprocal self-giving love emerges again: she has feasted on him (2:3), and now, at her invitation, he feasts on her (4:16—5:1). The newlyweds abandon themselves to the delights of love-making. The author's voice briefly intrudes to affirm them in their intoxicating joy: the goodness of committed sexual intimacy is to be celebrated. Sex does not need to be justified by any spiritual parallels. 'Let there be love,' as the band Oasis put it. 'In the image of God he created them; male and female… and indeed, it was very good' (Genesis 1:27, 31).

4 Lost and found again

Song of Songs 5:2—6:3

Romance brings emotional extremes. From the ecstatic bliss of the previous verses, we plunge without warning into an anxious scene, similar to 3:1–5. Again it is night-time; again the experience seems dream-like in its surreal strangeness and vividness. The woman hears her lover asking for access and intimacy; she seems uncertain or reluctant, or perhaps she is enjoying some teasing banter. Provoked, he tries harder, and suddenly she longs for him and moves to welcome him. But in a moment the game turns sour: she is shocked to find he has disappeared. She feels as if her very life is draining away (5:6). The vulnerabilities involved in loving rise to the surface, as the woman expresses agonies of uncertainty about the man's absence and its implications for their relationship. Absence makes the heart grow reckless: as in the earlier passage, she seeks him desperately in the streets, again meeting the city guardians; but this time she cannot find him and suffers physical abuse at their hands.

Provoked by questions from her (comforting or cruel?) companions (v. 9), the woman now conjures up her absent lover with her words, depicting him for all to see, with intriguing and emotionally evocative metaphors. To our surprise, it turns out that she does know where he is after all: he is present, enjoying the delights of his 'garden' (6:2), a metaphor for the woman herself. The passage ends with a renewed sense of his reassuring and intimate presence. There has been a disturbing crisis in the relationship, but, thankfully, anxiety is not all-consuming, nor does it have the final word.

Serenity and harmony pervade Howard Skempton's choral interpretations of the Song. No hint of discord disturbs the passages he chooses from the biblical text or the sublime voices that sing them. He gives an idealised vision of the beauty of love, inspiring and reassuring. However, the realities of love are more complex and demanding. The biblical Song repeatedly reflects the tensions that lovers experience, from the longing to be kissed (1:2) to the ambiguity of the final verse (8:14: is she telling him to give her space and leave her for a while, or to come close for further intimacy with her?). Love ebbs and flows restlessly; it is never complete and 'happy ever after'.

5 Delight and desire

Admiring descriptions of the loved one continue, this time from the man again. Three times he describes her: he delights in looking. As before, we find puzzling metaphors, which show us not so much what she looks like as how he sees her and feels about her.

The dance of mutuality continues in their dialogue, as both the lovers express their yearning and desire for each other (he in 7:6–9, she in 7:10—8:4). They both experience love as delightful yet also deeply disturbing, and they express its effects on them in different ways. We have heard her speak of being 'faint with love' (2:5; 5:8); she feels lovesick, left breathless by her feelings for him, craving sustenance—particularly his presence—to restore her. He, on the other hand, speaks of being ravished by her merest glance, overwhelmed and captivated by her eyes and beautiful hair (4:9; 6:5; 7:5). He is awestruck and feels a sense of losing control, which he finds both delightful and alarming. Issues of power and self-control arise for him. 'Her beauty and the moonlight overthrew you,' Leonard Cohen's 'Hallelujah' puts it, evoking King David's experience as he gazed at Bathsheba (2 Samuel 11:2–3).

Another repeated refrain in the Song is the solemn and enigmatic adjuration to the women of Jerusalem not to 'stir up or awaken love until it is ready' (2:7; 3:5; 8:4). This may be the woman (or the poet) simply insisting that the couple should not be disturbed in their more intimate moments, or perhaps it is a more general warning that love, in all its wonder and power, does not need to be stirred up but will rouse itself and arrive in its own good time.

Martin Smith's poignant 'Song of Solomon' touches on the biblical Song only slightly in a few phrases. It focuses repeatedly on the singer's need for the divine lover in the darkness and demands of life today. The biblical Song, in contrast, is focused not on the needs of the self but on the other: these lovers never say 'I need you' or even 'I love you', but instead marvel at 'how fair and pleasant you are' (7:6).

6 The power of love

As the Song draws towards its close, a different tone is briefly heard in a reflective comment about love in general, which may be crystallising the idea that the poet is most keen to convey (8:6–7).

Once again taking the initiative, the woman urges the man, 'Set me as a seal upon your heart.' A seal expressed the unique identity and commitment of its owner when impressed on to documents or clay. The woman longs for her life to be fused with his in an inseparable bond of mutual commitment. For lovers, boundaries seem to melt in a fusion of personalities, even as they remain distinct individuals.

Disturbing realities suddenly intrude, however—death, jealousy, fire and flood. Death is an enemy of love, and will eventually tear one of the lovers away; yet the Song proclaims that love will still triumph and live on. How does love endure after death? In the continuing feelings of the mourner, or in other loving relationships that the bereaved one will experience in due course? Perhaps those who have learned how to love will continue loving, one way or another. Or does love persist simply in the enduring vision of love presented by the poem itself? Let the reader decide.

Surging through these few concise lines is a sense of the awesome, irresistible power of love. Love is 'strong' and 'fierce', formidable—a flame that the mightiest floods cannot quench. Even the wealthiest find themselves powerless if they are foolish enough to try to buy it. The superlative 'raging flame' (v. 6) could be translated 'flame of Yah', using the shorter form of the divine name 'Yahweh'. Does this suggest that God is the source of the flame of love? It may indicate that the love that human beings can share arises from God and is a gift of God to humanity; human love is not to be worshipped but is to be modelled on the love found in God, and can in turn point to that higher and ultimate love. While singing of human love, the Song perhaps also whispers of God.

A passionate longing for more of God, often expressed in romantic terms, pervades the worship songs of Misty Edwards. Her evocation of Song 8:6–7 presents God relentlessly longing for human wholeheartedness, prompting a passionate response from the worshipper: 'until you and I are one'.

Guidelines

When Darlene Zschech writes of 'The kiss of heaven' and sings of 'worshipping the love of my life', romance and worship become blurred together—a tendency reflected by interpreters of the Song of Songs down the years, and by a number of contemporary song writers.

Sexual intimacy cannot be a means of encountering God: that would mean using (indeed, abusing) our human partner in order to achieve intimacy with someone else. But can it provide a helpful metaphor for encounter with God? Other biblical texts may shed light here. Some of the Old Testament prophets portray God as a husband (Isaiah 54:4–8; Jeremiah 2:2; Ezekiel 16; Hosea 1—3), but the metaphor they use tends to be one of traditional patriarchal marriage. The divine husband who loves is also the lord who commands his wayward people. The inequality and imbalance of power between these two parties may not be noticed by today's readers and worship song writers if they think more in terms of a romantic mutual love between equals. We may end up with a God who seems more approachable and less daunting, but is different from the God we meet in scripture. So if we use metaphors of loving intimacy and marriage in worship, we need to balance them with other pictures that emphasise the greatness, holiness and otherness of God.

For some of us, projecting romance on to our relationship with God might become an unhealthy distraction, diverting us from truly investing ourselves in human sexual intimacy, with all its joys and challenges. For others, the reverse might be true: do we resist spiritual interpretations of the Song of Songs because we are wary of exploring deeper intimacy with God, preferring to keep God at a safer distance?

The Song of Songs celebrates passionate intimacy in our closest human relationships. It also hints at a divine image in us and a divine source of our longing to love. Drawing closer to that source, that ultimate lover, can teach us how to be loved and how to give ourselves in love.

SONGS MENTIONED

Kate Bush, 'The Song of Solomon', from *The Red Shoes*, EMI, 1993.
Leonard Cohen, 'Hallelujah', from *Leonard Cohen: Live in Dublin*, Sony, 2014.
Misty Edwards, 'You won't relent', from *Relentless*, Forerunner, 2007.
Patrick Hawes, *Song of Songs*, Signum, 2009.

Oasis, 'Let there be love', from *Don't Believe the Truth*, Big Brother Recordings, 2005.

Howard Skempton, 'Rise up, my love' from *My Beloved's Voice: Sacred songs of love*, Signum, 2014.

Martin Smith, 'Song of Solomon', from *Back to the Start*, GloWorks, 2015.

Darlene Zschech, 'You are here', from *Change Your World*, INO, 2005.

FURTHER READING

Diane Bergant, *Song of Songs: The love poetry of scripture*, New City Press, 1998.

Charlie Cleverley, *Song of Songs: Exploring the divine romance*, Hodder, 2015.

Cheryl Exum, *Song of Songs*, Westminster John Knox, 2005.

Tom Gledhill, *The Message of the Song of Songs*, IVP, 1994.

Overleaf… Guidelines forthcoming issue | Author profile |
Recommended reading | Order and subscription forms

Guidelines forthcoming issue

DAVID SPRIGGS

1517 saw a very significant event take place, although initially it seemed ordinary enough. It was in that year, on 31 October, that Martin Luther 'posted' (that is, nailed to the door of the castle church at Wittenberg) his '95 Theses'. This was the normal way to start a theological discussion—the equivalent of blogging today, I suspect. The 95 Theses were written in Latin, not German, so Luther clearly had no intention of engaging ordinary people in his objections, but people soon were engaged. Many scholars see this event as the start of the Reformation proper.

We will be marking this 500th anniversary with three sets of notes that engage with Luther's thinking and spirituality. The first is by Professor Martyn Percy, Dean of Christ Church, Oxford. For Luther, the scriptures (not tradition or the church) were the primary source of knowledge about God, but the scriptures were far more than a source of ammunition for his theological battles. They were a great source of nourishment for his whole Christian life, and this was primarily true of the Psalms. Martyn writes:

Luther's Summaries of the Psalms *was published in 1532, as a companion to reading, singing and praying the Psalter... Luther believed in the 'natural sense of scriptures'—that they could be read and understood naturally, without aid or explanation. So he set himself the task of writing a commentary that was deliberately minimalist, so as to prevent his own text from coming between the person encountering the psalm and God's word through these scriptures.*

Under Martyn's expert and sympathetic guidance, we are allowed to experience the riches of Luther's devotional heart.

The second contribution is very different. It is written by Alistair Wilson, who teaches theology in Scotland. One of the key issues for the Reformation was the reality of 'justification'—what it was, what it accomplished and how it was accessed. The understanding that God 'justifies' sinners by his grace and through their faith in Christ alone was a shattering new truth for Luther. It was ascertained 'through meticulous exegetical engagement with Scripture' (S.W. Chung, *Alistair E. McGrath and Evangelical Theology*, Paternoster, 2003, p. 202). It was, of course, extremely controversial. Alistair Wilson introduces us to some of those key scriptures, illuminated by Luther's comments, and seeks to engage with the recent issues that scholars have uncovered about this profound and deeply challenging subject.

The final commemoration of Luther's 'posting' is by Mike Parsons, who has recently become a Commissioning Editor at BRF. Mike has taught systematic theology in Australia (and you can find out more about him in the next issue of *Guidelines*). He shows us yet another side to Luther, helping us to appreciate Luther's understanding of and practice of prayer.

In the next issue we also have Nigel Wright completing his contributions on Matthew's Gospel, Matthew van Duyvenbode on Thessalonians, our respected friend Alec Gilmore on Numbers, and Mark Scarlata (a new writer for us) exploring insights for leaders from the life of Moses. Then, of course, we have not neglected the Advent season. Sarah Beresford focuses on 'God's Advent call', Jeremy Duff unpacks the incarnation in John's Gospel, while I explore some of the rich Christian words within the Christmas story in Luke 2:8–20.

This issue is marking a very special anniversary but it is also full of great biblical riches. Please encourage your friends to get hold of a copy, as well as reading it with profit yourselves.

Author profile: John Leach

I have two early memories of the Bible. When I was five years old, my dad had a 'Damascus road' conversion, and from then on we went to our local Baptist church, morning, afternoon and evening. Our diet was up to 45 minutes of preaching, most of which went completely over my head, but I loved snuggling up to my mum and looking at pictures like 'Saul as a boy watching the ships pull into Tarsus' in my Authorised Version. So, from an early age, the Bible was associated for me with warmth and security.

Later on, I can remember being fascinated by the book of Revelation with its dragons, beasts, and trumpets, which seemed exciting to a young teenage boy. Again, I had no idea what it was all about, but it felt like fun.

I was nurtured, first in the Baptist Church, and later in the Anglican, in churches that took the scriptures seriously. A major influence on me was a teaching series imaginatively called 'Through the Bible in just over a year', where each week we had two sermons, one on the background to each book and the other on its application to life today. The series gave me a great overview of the big sweep of the Bible and reinforced the message that the Bible should be central to the life of Christian discipleship.

I approached academic study in the 1970s with some trepidation, having heard that my college was one of the most liberal in the country and delighted in destroying the faith of students, particularly 'fundamentalist' ones. As I began to study original languages, however, I found that my faith, rather than crumbling, was renewed and strengthened as I explored the scriptures at a new level. I fell in love with the Bible even more passionately.

Around this time I also encountered the teaching ministry of David Pawson. While I didn't agree with his take on everything, I loved his ambition to teach through every book of the Bible. My own preaching ministry since ordination has, I hope, been characterised by faithfulness to the scriptures, in a way that takes seriously the best efforts of academic theologians. Most of them, I discovered with some surprise, were just Christians like me, trying to make sense of what the Bible actually taught.

Now I work in a diocesan discipleship team, where I find that engagement with scripture is a key to discipleship, and the lack of it a major inhibiting factor. It saddens me to see how many churchgoers have little experience of studying the Bible for themselves, or indeed of having heard it taught systematically. I am currently thinking about 'temple versus synagogue' as a model for church, particularly in the more rural areas of our nation, where we are trying to sustain thousands of mini-cathedrals with neither the resources nor the skills to do so. What would the church look like if, like the Jews in the synagogue, we simply gathered around the word to seek wisdom about practical discipleship, and to encourage and build one another up in our faith? Add to that the missing ingredient of the Spirit, and we would have worship that more closely reflected our New Testament glimpses of the first Christians gathering together.

My final thought is the truth of the old adage that, as Christians, we stand under the authority of scripture rather than sitting in judgement over it. Most of the current controversies in the church stem, I believe, from our attempts to disagree with and rewrite the Bible to make it more politically correct, more acceptable in our current culture. If the Bible challenges something in me or in my culture, I believe I have to listen carefully to it rather than simply disagreeing with it.

I count it a privilege to write for The Bible Reading Fellowship, and I hope that others will be inspired to love the scriptures as much as I do.

Experiencing
Christ's Love
Establishing a life of worship, prayer,
study, service and reflection
John Twisleton

An extract from
Experiencing Christ's Love

In *Experiencing Christ's Love*, author John Twisleton reminds us of Jesus' gracious challenge to love God with heart, soul and mind, and to love our neighbour and ourselves. Against the backdrop of the message of God's unconditional love in Jesus Christ, he delivers a wake-up call to the basic Christian patterns of worship, prayer, study, service and reflection. The following extract is taken from the first chapter.

First love: worship

'You shall love the Lord your God with all your heart' (Matthew 22:37). I am intrigued by worship. It's been around since before the world was made and will continue after its predicted meltdown. There's something awesome about connecting the heart of the universe with the human heart and lifting hearts together towards what is ultimate. It's extravagant, lacks restraint and goes beyond reason in the way love is bound to do... In it we touch the face of God and something of him rubs off on us: 'Look to him and be radiant' (Psalm 34:5). When I was a teenager I found a remarkable place where Sunday services were like heaven to me. It was something totally different. The priest seemed like a saint and the unselfconscious ceremonial, music and preaching made heaven above real and brought radiance to faces around me. I sought and found a word in the dictionary that summed it up—'numinous' or filled with a sense of the supernatural, a sense that up to then I had not seen exercised.

Being so intrigued by worship, I'm writing this book partly as a call to recapture that sense of the supernatural which worship in the western church seems to have lost. As someone drawn to God by the supernatural in worship I can understand why church attendance is in decline when so much of what we call celebration feels so earthbound. To me, God has sameness, yes, but is also utterly different in his holiness. When I worship on Sunday I say, 'Holy, holy, holy, Lord, God of power and might' and expect to leave church different because of expectations of God, worship and the church raised all those years ago.

Suspicion of otherworldliness has grown on account of religious fanatics, unhinged through excessive irrationality, who see God as terrifyingly different, with the sameness to us who bear his image lost. Religion like money, power or sex is God-given but gets man-handled! The etymology of the word 'religion' is linked to the Latin *ligare*, meaning 'to bind'. I am unapologetically religious—regularly attending Sunday worship—because I want to keep re-binding myself to God and his people. So much of my life loosens me from what's ultimate, from the love of God. I need to continually bind myself back to God through the five loves Jesus describes in his summary of religion: '"You shall love the Lord your God with all your heart, and with all your soul, and with all your mind." This is the greatest and first commandment. And a second is like it: "You shall love your neighbour as yourself"' (Matthew 22:37–39)...

Experiencing Christ's love

How do you see God? Maybe he's close to you as a new Christian but the warmth of the first encounter is cooling. Or, like the mature Christians of Laodicea referred to in Revelation 3:16, 'you are lukewarm, and neither hot nor cold'. Either way, you are seeking to find strategies to know the love of God for real, inasmuch as it depends on you. The good news we'll come back to again and again is rooted in a vision of God who's 'always more ready to hear than we to pray and to give more than either we desire or deserve'. That lovely phrase from the Collect is read as part of worship day by day for a week every summer and, as with so many worship texts, acts to speak to us and remind us, as well as God, for whom all human worship is unnecessary reminder.

Like the Collect, this book is a reminder of love, being loved and loving, for which words matter less than attitudes and deeds, so the book is at heart a reminder to stick at loving God in the five aspects Jesus Christ invites, knowing 'we love because he first loved us' (1 John 4:19).

No one writes more eloquently about the love of God in Jesus Christ than the apostle Paul whose writings are a substantial part of the New Testament. Even his words, with all their force, crack as they address the love of God shown us in Jesus Christ. When, for example, Paul speaks to the Ephesians of 'knowing the love of Christ which passes knowledge', what does he mean? There's real ambiguity about the phrase 'knowing the love of Christ' and it's helpful to examine it.

Does Paul mean God's love for us? Or the blessings that come from our loving God? Or is it God's love in Christ for all that is, that he draws us into?

These are three ways of interpreting that phrase 'knowing the love of Christ' and they are all precious insights. To know the Son of God loved us and gave himself for us is, as Paul puts it in Galatians 2:20, our greatest motivator. To love God in the face of Jesus Christ is a blessing, since our devotion to him is God's gift passing earthly knowledge, and as Jesus himself says in Matthew 5:6, wanting most of all what God wants will satisfy us fully. To know the love of Christ, thirdly, is to sympathise with and enter into God's compassion towards all people and all things, shown in the perpetual gift of his Son Jesus Christ.

I don't know which of the three interpretations of 'knowing the love of Christ' is right—it's probably all three! We'll follow them chapter by chapter as variations on a theme: downward love for us from God, upward love from us to him and outward love from God and believers to the world. Whatever Paul meant by 'knowing the love of Christ which passes knowledge', I want that love, from him, for him and with him and I would that were so for all of us and for the whole creation.

Christianity starts with God's love for us in Christ, and our response follows, a disciplined response which bears fruit in bringing others to experience Christ's love. That response is corporate, a receiving and giving out, with all followers of Jesus in this world and the next. It is corporate because the many-sided love of God can only be grasped 'with all the saints' (Ephesians 3:18). This truth is captured eloquently by Baron Friedrich von Hügel when he writes of the Christian calling to become 'a great living cloth of gold with not only the woof going from God to man [sic] and from man to God, but also the warp going from man to man... and thus the primary and full Bride of Christ never is, nor can be, the individual man at prayer, but only this complete organism of all the faithful people throughout time and space'... When I go to church I go to worship and engage with God in Christ, present in bread and wine, in preaching, prayer and fellowship. Sometimes the sermon's dull, the sacrament feels empty or the prayers sound flat. One way or another—and it's good there are a number of ways—Christ makes his presence real to me. Sometimes it's in a conversation or kind action I experience afterwards involving a fellow Christian. That reminds me that my commitment to worship isn't just as an individual but is part of something much bigger, that 'great living cloth of gold' which is the church, the 'complete organism of all the faithful people throughout space and time'.

John Twisleton is a Sussex priest, theologian and pastor. He broadcasts regularly on Premier Radio. To order a copy of his book, please visit brfonline.org.uk or use the order form on page 149.

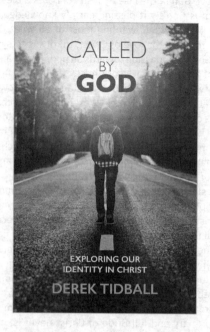

CALLED
BY
GOD

EXPLORING OUR
IDENTITY IN CHRIST

DEREK TIDBALL

In an age in which it seems that everyone is concerned with their own identity, popular author and conference speaker Derek Tidball examines twelve key New Testament passages which go right to the heart of the matter. Identity for Christians, the Bible says, is rooted in who we are in Jesus Christ. Reflecting on Christian vocation, the author draws us back to see how the Bible speaks about the nature of who we have become by faith. Each chapter ends with questions, opening the reader to thoughtful and practical response.

Called by God
Exploring our identity in Christ
Derek Tidball
978 0 85746 530 6 £7.99
brfonline.org.uk

God's Belongers should transform our thinking about what it means to belong to church. David Walker offers a fourfold model of belonging: through relationship, through place, through events, and through activities. He shows how 'belonging' can encompass a far wider group of people than those who attend weekly services, opening up creative opportunities for mission in today's world.

God's Belongers
How people engage with God today and how the church can help
David Walker
978 0 85746 467 5   £8.99
brfonline.org.uk

Combining missional vision with practical advice, these resources, written by Laura Treneer, give you the tools you need to transform your church communications. Ideal for church teams who want to reach their communities effectively, and a perfect gift for church leaders and volunteers who are short on time but need fast relevant advice.

Church Online: Websites
978 0 85746 552 8 £3.99

Church Online: Social media
978 0 85746 557 3 £3.99

Church from the Outside
978 0 85746 553 5 £3.99

Church from the Inside
978 0 85746 554 2 £3.99

brfonline.org.uk

To order

Online: brfonline.org.uk
Telephone: +44 (0)1865 319700
Mon–Fri 9.15–17.30

Delivery times within the UK are normally
15 working days. Prices are correct at the time of
going to press but may change without prior notice.

Title	Price	Qty	Total
Reproducing Churches	£12.99		
Being Messy, Being Church	£9.99		
Experiencing God's Love	£7.99		
Called by God	£7.99		
God's Belongers	£8.99		
Church Online: Websites	£3.99		
Church Online: Social media	£3.99		
Church from the Outside: Displays, noticeboards, invitations, PR	£3.99		
Church from the Inside: Welcome, news sheets, magazines, stories	£3.99		

POSTAGE AND PACKING CHARGES			
Order value	UK	Europe	Rest of world
Under £7.00	£1.25	£3.00	£5.50
£7.00–£29.99	£2.25	£5.50	£10.00
£30.00 and over	FREE	Prices on request	

Total value of books	
Postage and packing	
Total for this order	

Please complete in BLOCK CAPITALS

Title .... First name/initials .... Surname...................................

Address...

....Postcode...........................

Acc. No. .... Telephone ....

Email...

Please keep me informed about BRF's books and resources ❏ by email ❏ by post
Please keep me informed about the wider work of BRF ❏ by email ❏ by post

Method of payment

❏ Cheque (made payable to BRF) ❏ MasterCard / Visa

Card no. ❏❏❏❏ ❏❏❏❏ ❏❏❏❏ ❏❏❏❏ ❏❏❏❏

Valid from [M][M] [Y][Y] Expires [M][M] [Y][Y] Security code* ❏❏❏

Last 3 digits on the reverse of the card

Signature* .... Date .... /............ /............
*ESSENTIAL IN ORDER TO PROCESS YOUR ORDER

Please return this form to: BRF, 15 The Chambers, Vineyard, Abingdon OX14 3FE | enquiries@brf.org.uk
To read our terms and find out about cancelling your order, please visit brfonline.org.uk/terms.

The Bible Reading Fellowship (BRF) is a Registered Charity (233280)

How to encourage Bible reading in your church

The Bible Reading Fellowship has been helping individuals connect with the Bible for over 90 years. We want to support churches as they seek to encourage church members into regular Bible reading.

Order a Bible reading resources pack

This pack is designed to give your church the tools to publicise our Bible reading notes. It includes:

- Sample Bible reading notes for your congregation to try.
- Publicity resources, including a poster.
- A church magazine feature about Bible reading notes.

The pack is free, but we welcome a £5 donation to cover the cost of postage. If you require a pack to be sent outside the UK or require a specific number of sample Bible reading notes, please contact us for postage costs. More information about what the current pack contains is available on our website.

How to order and find out more

- Visit **biblereadingnotes.org.uk/for-churches**
- Telephone BRF on +44 (0)1865 319700 Mon–Fri 9.15–17.30
- Write to us at BRF, 15 The Chambers, Vineyard, Abingdon OX14 3FE

Keep informed about our latest initiatives

We are continuing to develop resources to help churches encourage people into regular Bible reading, wherever they are on their journey. Join our email list at **biblereadingnotes.org.uk/helpingchurches** to stay informed about the latest initiatives that your church could benefit from.

Introduce a friend to our notes

We can send information about our notes and current prices for you to pass on. Please contact us.

Transforming Lives and Communities

The Bible Reading Fellowship is a charity that is passionate about making a difference through the Christian faith. We want to see lives and communities transformed through our creative programmes and resources for individuals, churches and schools. We are doing this by resourcing:

- **Christian growth and understanding of the Bible.** Through our Bible reading notes, books, digital resources, Quiet Days and other events, we're resourcing individuals, groups and leaders in churches for their own spiritual journey and for their ministry.

- **Church outreach in the local community.** BRF is the home of three programmes that churches are embracing to great effect as they seek to engage with their local communities: Messy Church, Who Let The Dads Out? and The Gift of Years.

- **Teaching Christianity in primary schools.** Our Barnabas in Schools team is working with primary-aged children and their teachers, enabling them to explore Christianity creatively and confidently within the school curriculum.

- **Children's and family ministry.** Through our Barnabas in Churches and Faith in Homes websites and published resources, we're working with churches and families, enabling children under 11, and the adults working with them, to explore Christianity creatively and bring the Bible alive.

Do you share our vision?

Sales of our books and Bible reading notes cover the cost of producing them. However, our other programmes are funded primarily by donations, grants and legacies. If you share our vision, would you help us to transform even more lives and communities? Your prayers and financial support are vital for the work that we do.

- You could support BRF's ministry with a one-off gift or regular donation (using the response form on page 153).
- You could consider making a bequest to BRF in your will (page 152).
- You could encourage your church to support BRF as part of your church's giving to home mission—perhaps focusing on a specific area of our ministry, or a particular member of our Barnabas team.
- Most important of all, you could support BRF with your prayers.

Make a lasting difference through a gift in your will

For almost a century The Bible Reading Fellowship (BRF) has been able to do amazing things thanks to the generosity of those who have supported us through gifts in wills. Today our creative programmes impact the lives of thousands of individuals across the UK and overseas.

One such programme is The Gift of Years, which aims to improve the spiritual lives of older people across the UK. Through local churches we are growing a network of Anna Chaplains who deliver spiritual care services to older people of strong, little or no faith.

The late Joyce Barrett was visited regularly by Anna Chaplains at her care home in Hampshire. Joyce often shared stories from her life and, over time, showed an openness and willingness to explore life's big questions. On one occasion an Anna Chaplain was delivering a Communion service at her care home. This sparked a conversation that would result in Joyce becoming a Christian at the age of 89.

Standing alongside teenagers at her baptism service, Joyce was, and still is, a powerful witness to the fact that it's never too late to follow Christ. When Joyce died a few months later, all three Anna Chaplains who had cared for her took part in service of thanksgiving for her life.

If you share our passion for making a difference through the Christian faith, please consider leaving a gift in your will to BRF. Gifts in wills are an important source of income for us and they don't need to be huge to make a real difference. For every £1 we receive, we invest 95p back into charitable activities. Just imagine what we could do over the next century with your help.

For further information about making a gift to BRF in your will, please visit **brf.org.uk** or contact Sophie on +44 (0)1865 319700 or email giving@brf.org.uk.

Whatever you can do or give, we thank you for your support.

SHARING OUR VISION—MAKING A GIFT

I would like to make a gift to support BRF. Please use my gift for:

☐ where it is needed most ☐ Barnabas Children's Ministry

☐ Messy Church ☐ Who Let The Dads Out? ☐ The Gift of Years

Title	First name/initials	Surname

Address

Postcode

Email

Telephone

Signature	Date

giftaid it You can add an extra 25p to every £1 you give.

Please treat as Gift Aid donations all qualifying gifts of money made

☐ today, ☐ in the past four years, ☐ and in the future.

I am a UK taxpayer and understand that if I pay less Income Tax and/or Capital Gains Tax in the current tax year than the amount of Gift Aid claimed on all my donations, it is my responsibility to pay any difference.

☐ My donation does not qualify for Gift Aid.

Please notify BRF if you want to cancel this Gift Aid declaration, change your name or home address, or no longer pay sufficient tax on your income and/or capital gains.

Please complete other side of form ➡

Please return this form to:
BRF, 15 The Chambers, Vineyard, Abingdon OX14 3FE

The Bible Reading Fellowship is a Registered Charity (233280)

SHARING OUR VISION—MAKING A GIFT

Regular giving

By Direct Debit:

☐ I would like to make a regular gift of £ [   ] per month/quarter/year.
Please also complete the Direct Debit instruction on page 159.

By Standing Order:

Please contact Priscilla Kew, tel. +44 (0)1235 462305; giving@brf.org.uk

One-off donation

Please accept my gift of:

☐ £10 ☐ £50 ☐ £100 Other £ [   ]

by (delete as appropriate):

☐ Cheque/Charity Voucher payable to 'BRF'

☐ MasterCard/Visa/Debit card/Charity card

Name on card [   ]

Card no. [ ][ ][ ][ ] [ ][ ][ ][ ] [ ][ ][ ][ ] [ ][ ][ ][ ]

Valid from [M][M][Y][Y] Expires [M][M][Y][Y]

Security code* [ ][ ][ ] *Last 3 digits on the reverse of the card
ESSENTIAL IN ORDER TO PROCESS YOUR PAYMENT

Signature [   ] Date [   ]

We like to acknowledge all donations. However, if you do not wish to receive
an acknowledgement, please tick here ☐

↻ Please complete other side of form

Please return this form to:
BRF, 15 The Chambers, Vineyard, Abingdon OX14 3FE

BRF

The Bible Reading Fellowship is a Registered Charity (233280)

GL0217

Please note our subscription rates, current until April 2018:

Individual subscriptions
covering 3 issues for under 5 copies, payable in advance
(including postage & packing):

	UK	Europe	Rest of world
Guidelines	£16.50	£24.60	£28.50
Guidelines 3-year subscription (9 issues)	£45.00	N/A	N/A

Group subscriptions
covering 3 issues for 5 copies or more, sent to **one** UK address (post free):

Guidelines	£13.20 per set of 3 issues p.a.

Please note that the annual billing period for group subscriptions runs from 1 May to 30 April.

Overseas group subscription rates
Available on request. Please email enquiries@brf.org.uk.

Copies may also be obtained from Christian bookshops:

Guidelines	£4.40 per copy

All our Bible reading notes can be ordered online by visiting
biblereadingnotes.org.uk/subscriptions

For information about our other Bible reading notes,
and apps for iPhone and iPod touch, visit
biblereadingnotes.org.uk

GUIDELINES INDIVIDUAL SUBSCRIPTION FORM

All our Bible reading notes can be ordered online by visiting
biblereadingnotes.org.uk/subscriptions

☐ I would like to take out a subscription:

Title .... First name/initials .... Surname ....

Address ....

.... Postcode ....

Telephone .... Email ....

Please send *Guidelines* beginning with the September 2017 / January 2018 / May 2018
issue (*delete as appropriate*):

(*please tick box*)

	UK	Europe	Rest of world
Guidelines	☐ £16.50	☐ £24.60	☐ £28.50
Guidelines 3-year subscription	☐ £45.00	N/A	N/A

Total enclosed £ .... (cheques should be made payable to 'BRF')

Please charge my MasterCard / Visa ☐ Debit card ☐ with £ ....

Card no. ☐☐☐☐ ☐☐☐☐ ☐☐☐☐ ☐☐☐☐

Valid from ☐☐ ☐☐ Expires ☐☐ ☐☐ Security code* ☐☐☐

Last 3 digits on the reverse of the card

Signature* .... Date .... /....... /.......

*ESSENTIAL IN ORDER TO PROCESS YOUR PAYMENT

To set up a Direct Debit, please also complete the Direct Debit instruction on page 159
and return it to BRF with this form.

Please return this form with the appropriate payment to:
BRF, 15 The Chambers, Vineyard, Abingdon OX14 3FE

To read our terms and find out about cancelling your order, please visit **brfonline.org.uk/terms**.

The Bible Reading Fellowship (BRF) is a Registered Charity (233280)

GL0217

GUIDELINES GIFT SUBSCRIPTION FORM

☐ I would like to give a gift subscription (please provide both names and addresses):

Title .... First name/initials .... Surname ....

Address ....

.... Postcode ....

Telephone .... Email ....

Gift subscription name ....

Gift subscription address ....

.... Postcode ....

Gift message (20 words max. or include your own gift card):

....

....

Please send *Guidelines* beginning with the September 2017 / January 2018 / May 2018 issue (*delete as appropriate*):

(*please tick box*)

	UK	Europe	Rest of world
Guidelines	☐ £16.50	☐ £24.60	☐ £28.50
Guidelines 3-year subscription	☐ £45.00	N/A	N/A

Total enclosed £ .... (cheques should be made payable to 'BRF')

Please charge my MasterCard / Visa ☐ Debit card ☐ with £ ....

Card no. ☐☐☐☐ ☐☐☐☐ ☐☐☐☐ ☐☐☐☐

Valid from ☐☐ ☐☐ Expires ☐☐ ☐☐ Security code* ☐☐☐

Last 3 digits on the reverse of the card

Signature* .... Date .... / .... / ....

*ESSENTIAL IN ORDER TO PROCESS YOUR PAYMENT

To set up a Direct Debit, please also complete the Direct Debit instruction on page 159 and return it to BRF with this form.

Please return this form with the appropriate payment to:
BRF, 15 The Chambers, Vineyard, Abingdon OX14 3FE

To read our terms and find out about cancelling your order, please visit brfonline.org.uk/terms.

The Bible Reading Fellowship (BRF) is a Registered Charity (233280)

DIRECT DEBIT PAYMENT

You can pay for your annual subscription to our Bible reading notes using Direct Debit. You need only give your bank details once, and the payment is made automatically every year until you cancel it. If you would like to pay by Direct Debit, please use the form opposite, entering your BRF account number under 'Reference number'.

You are fully covered by the Direct Debit Guarantee:

The Direct Debit Guarantee

- This Guarantee is offered by all banks and building societies that accept instructions to pay Direct Debits.

- If there are any changes to the amount, date or frequency of your Direct Debit, The Bible Reading Fellowship will notify you 10 working days in advance of your account being debited or as otherwise agreed. If you request The Bible Reading Fellowship to collect a payment, confirmation of the amount and date will be given to you at the time of the request.

- If an error is made in the payment of your Direct Debit, by The Bible Reading Fellowship or your bank or building society, you are entitled to a full and immediate refund of the amount paid from your bank or building society.

- If you receive a refund you are not entitled to, you must pay it back when The Bible Reading Fellowship asks you to.

- You can cancel a Direct Debit at any time by simply contacting your bank or building society. Written confirmation may be required. Please also notify us.

GL0217

The Bible Reading Fellowship

Instruction to your bank or building society to pay by Direct Debit

Please fill in the whole form using a ballpoint pen and return it to:
BRF, 15 The Chambers, Vineyard, Abingdon OX14 3FE

Service User Number: | 5 | 5 | 8 | 2 | 2 | 9 |

Name and full postal address of your bank or building society

To: The Manager	Bank/Building Society
Address	
	Postcode

Name(s) of account holder(s)

Branch sort code

Bank/Building Society account number

Reference number

Instruction to your Bank/Building Society

Please pay The Bible Reading Fellowship Direct Debits from the account detailed
in this instruction, subject to the safeguards assured by the Direct Debit Guarantee.
I understand that this instruction may remain with The Bible Reading Fellowship
and, if so, details will be passed electronically to my bank/building society.

Signature(s)

Banks and Building Societies may not accept Direct Debit instructions for some types
of account.

This page is left blank for your notes.